The Scandal of
the Evangelical College

The Scandal of the Evangelical College

Why Christian Higher Education Fails the Church

MARTIN SPENCE

CASCADE *Books* • Eugene, Oregon

THE SCANDAL OF THE EVANGELICAL COLLEGE
Why Christian Higher Education Fails the Church

Copyright © 2025 Martin Spence. All rights reserved. Except for brief quotations in critical publications or reviews, no part of this book may be reproduced in any manner without prior written permission from the publisher. Write: Permissions, Wipf and Stock Publishers, 199 W. 8th Ave., Suite 3, Eugene, OR 97401.

Cascade Books
An Imprint of Wipf and Stock Publishers
199 W. 8th Ave., Suite 3
Eugene, OR 97401

www.wipfandstock.com

PAPERBACK ISBN: 978-1-6667-8928-7
HARDCOVER ISBN: 978-1-6667-8929-4
EBOOK ISBN: 978-1-6667-8930-0

Cataloguing-in-Publication data:

Names: Spence, Martin, author

Title: The scandal of the evangelical college : why Christian higher education fails the church / Martin Spence.

Description: Eugene, OR: Cascade Books, 2025 | Includes bibliographical references.

Identifiers: ISBN 978-1-6667-8928-7 (paperback) | ISBN 978-1-6667-8929-4 (hardcover) | ISBN 978-1-6667-8930-0 (ebook)

Subjects: LCSH: Education (Christian theology). | Theology—Study and teaching.

Classification: BT738.17 S68 2025 (paperback) | BT738.17 (ebook)

VERSION NUMBER 06/27/25

"Evangelical colleges and universities have lost touch with the church, and it is indeed a scandal. Administrators and boards of these institutions *must* come to grips with Martin Spence's arguments. All those connected to Christian higher education need to read this book."
—JOHN FEA,
distinguished professor of American history, Messiah University

"The 'scandal' of the evangelical college, according to Martin Spence, lies in its conflation of faith and individual piety. This results in its attempt to bring a Christian 'worldview' into a predetermined curriculum. Spence's compelling alternative lets us see education as an ecclesial vocation that transforms faith into a shared way of life at once social, political, and economic. His analysis opens the imagination to how the Christian college might yet offer a rich alternative to the domesticated faith of late modernity."
—ELIZABETH NEWMAN,
adjunct professor of theology, Duke Divinity School

"Although many evangelical colleges trumpet their orthodoxy, Martin Spence rightly points out that there's more than one way to give in to the secular spirit of the age. Rather than serving the church, the mission of evangelical colleges largely matches their secular counterparts: preparing individuals to serve the market economy. Spence's compelling critique and vision for moving forward makes this a must-read for this time of great upheaval in Christian higher education."
—BRANSON PARLER,
professor of theology, The Foundry

"In this book, Martin Spence makes an excellent scholarly contribution that demonstrates the multidimensional and multifaceted nature of secularization in Christian higher education. Spence concludes by offering practical suggestions on how Christian higher education can go beyond being reactionary to the amoral demands of the marketplace by being visionary through the building of alignment between Christian higher education and the church community. Doing so would enable rooting the practice of Christian transformation at the grassroots level, where ordinary lay people could be effectively reached."
—SAMUEL ZALANGA,
professor emeritus of sociology, Bethel University

Contents

Chapter 1	The Scandal Identified	1
Chapter 2	Christ and the Catalog	18
Chapter 3	The Disintegration of Faith and Learning	45
Chapter 4	The College of the Evangelical Scandal	71
Chapter 5	Doing College for the People of God	96

Bibliography | 121

Chapter 1

The Scandal Identified

THIS BOOK IS ABOUT the type of Christian colleges that make up the Council for Christian Colleges and Universities (CCCU). The CCCU was created in 1976 to represent the interests of Christian colleges to the United States federal government. The CCCU consists of around 150 Christian colleges and universities in North America, with an additional thirty worldwide, collectively educating over 500,000 students and employing 90,000 faculty and staff.[1] To its members it offers numerous resources, grants, and networking opportunities, as well as a measure of common identity.

I am going to describe these CCCU institutions as "Evangelical" because they bear the hallmarks of the form of piety and praxis commonly known as *Evangelicalism*.[2] The "Evangelical" ethos emerged within

---

1. CCCU, "About"; Ringenberg, *Christian College*, 198–201.

2. Ringenberg calls these colleges "orthodox" and stresses the intentionality with which they maintain a Christian worldview (Ringenberg, *Christian College*, 211). Burtchaell, following David Riesman, calls them "committed Christian" (Burtchaell, *Dying of the Light*, 743). I am aware that there is a spectrum of religious constituencies within the CCCU, and that the term "Evangelical" is sometimes reserved for a *subset* of CCCU colleges, particularly those without roots in a particular denominational or confessional community. However, I am using the term more generically for three reasons. First, because the binding core of CCCU schools reflects key "Evangelical" priorities (as described in the next paragraph). Second, because as Christian colleges have broadened from their denominational pasts they have often found in the moniker "Evangelical" a useful catch-all under which can shelter a range of students and faculty. Third, the book would become unwieldly if the fine distinctions between different emphases intruded too heavily. Readers may of course adapt and modify my observations in light of their own denominational and religious context. On the tendency to adopt the term "Evangelical" as colleges broadened their student constituency, see Douglas Jacobsen, "History

1

eighteenth-century North Atlantic Protestantism. It is a form of piety that stresses the importance of a dynamic relationship between the individual and Christ, emphasizes the authority of Scripture, and asserts that Christian faith should impel believers to lives of sanctified action.[3] This trinity of priorities is reflected in the values that the CCCU identifies as hallmarks of its member institutions. CCCU colleges are committed "to hir[ing] as full-time faculty members and administrators only persons who profess faith in Jesus Christ," "to integrating the Holy Scriptures" into all aspects of collegiate life, and to "graduating students who live and share the Gospel in word and deed [and] who live out Christian virtues such as love, courage, and humility in every aspect of their lives."[4]

"Evangelicalism" refers not only a set of spiritual convictions but also to a social movement. Although the Evangelical movement has no official organization, leadership, or creed, it nonetheless has subtle means of policing its borders. Evangelicalism has always adopted linguistic boundary markers, such as "born again" or "Bible-believing," that have attempted to distinguish "real" from "nominal" Christian faith. The pervasive claim of CCCU institutions to be "Christ-centered" is one such totemic marker of Evangelical identity. This coded phrase signals spiritual intensity, orthodoxy, and zeal. It is deployed to put a measure of conceptual distance between CCCU institutions and other religious colleges and is intended to signal that Christian faith and devotion is not just a tradition or inheritance but is all-encompassing and foundational.

CCCU colleges make bold claims for the depth and profundity of their religious identity. Such claims naturally invite correspondingly strong scrutiny. Do Evangelical colleges live up to their own claim that Christ is at the center of all they do? Or has the Evangelical college "domesticated," "dumbed down," and reduced the idea of Christ-centeredness "to little

---

and Character of Messiah College, 1909–1995," in Hughes and Adrian, eds., *Models*, 341; and Paul Toews, "Religious Idealism and Academic Vocation at Fresno Pacific College," in Hughes and Adrian, eds., *Models*, 237.

3. The literature on Evangelicalism, including debates about the very definition of the term, is vast. Useful starting points for nonspecialists include: Sweeney, *American Evangelical Story*; Kidd, *Who Is An Evangelical?*; Noll et al., eds. *Evangelicals*; Carter and Porter, *Turning Points in the History of American Evangelicalism*.

4. CCCU, "Our Institutions." I am aware that these priorities are also shared with colleges that are not members of the CCCU. Readers are at liberty to apply my commentary throughout this book to any college to which it seems apposite! See Gehrz, "Christian Higher Ed Is Not the CCCU."

more than an unctuous platitude"?[5] In this book I am going to argue that despite (and perhaps even *because of*) the claims made by Evangelical colleges about their Christian character, they are in fact scandalously secularized institutions. This is an obviously provocative claim. Some readers may consider it absurd. After all, most Christian college campuses are a hive of religious activity, including chapels, Bible studies, and mission trips. Their prevalent stringent moral codes—no drinking, no smoking, no sex—are a far cry from the average American higher education institution. The hiring policies, public discourse, and self-understanding of the Evangelical college are clearly rooted in a distinct religious identity. Most importantly, each Evangelical college insists that the education offered on its campus is pervaded by Christian perspectives and infused with faith. And yet, as Wayne Barnard has observed, while "the essential parts exist at our CCCU institutions for fully developed, faith-filled campus cultures . . . the whole is always greater than the sum of its parts . . . We are easily lulled into believing that because all of the right ingredients exist, Christian faith will always inform, and transform our campus culture."[6] The Christ-centered components of the Christian college do not always add up to a Christocentric whole. This book attempts to explain this thesis and to propose a remedy.

This is an iconoclastic text. It arises from my own frustrations working in and reading about Evangelical higher education. Since I have not experienced life in most Christian colleges, I concede that not all my criticisms will apply equally to every institution. There will be ways in which institutions and individuals might be able to defend themselves against my arguments. I also admit that I have probably picked the worst-case scenarios rather than the best. Finally, I confess that I am over-reliant on written literature rather than observed case studies. Despite these caveats I suspect that my experience exemplifies enough of the issues at play in Evangelical higher education that it will resonate with at least some of my readers for some of the time.

I have been working on this book sporadically for several years. The opportunity to bring it to completion came with the COVID-19 crisis and my (only somewhat reluctant) sequestration in the basement. At the start of the crisis it felt wrong to resume work on this project; wrong to indulge in lofty critique against institutions that were, for good or ill, suffering. But as

---

5. Litfin, *Conceiving the Christian College*, 36.

6. Wayne Barnard, "Faith and Campus Culture: Living and Learning in the Questions," in Joeckel and Chesnes, eds., *Christian College Phenomenon*, 104.

the pandemic wore on, it became clear that conversations about the world that might be born after the pandemic receded were beginning. This storm has washed away the topsoil of our routinized resignation to normalcy and exposed hitherto subaltern anxieties. It has also stirred aspirations for renewal and reform that in calmer seas would be dismissed as improbable and impracticable. Reflecting on the experience of the pandemic, history professor Chris Gehrz has ruminated that he is less afraid that the crisis will lead to the closure of his Christian college and more that "it will try to stay open *by drifting further from its core mission* as a liberal arts college that bears witness to Jesus Christ: seeking the truth found in him, transforming students in his likeness, and spreading his kingdom."[7] I share Gehrz's fear that one route forward will indeed be a quickening of the phenomenon that I diagnose in this book, and that the scandal of the Evangelical college will become a tragedy. And yet this is a moment when revisionist and iconoclastic visions for change have been moved from being utopian to becoming possible and even necessary. To quote Gehrz again: "I can't shake the feeling that preserving the status quo of Christian higher education has required that we linger in houses whose welcome was always conditional or incomplete ... at this point, I'd rather contemplate radical leaps than accept more comfortable steps that end with us sliding into something worse than irrelevance."[8] Amen.

"WHAT MAKES A CHRISTIAN COLLEGE SO SPECIAL?"[9]

What is the point of the Evangelical college? Answers to this question are luxuriant but as I have surveyed the tomes written about Christian higher education and reflected on my own personal experience of the Evangelical college, I became aware of a serious lacuna in this discourse. Very few people who have explained the purpose and priorities of the Evangelical college have had much to say about how it might serve the church. As Douglas Harink observes, there has been a "marginalization of the Church in shaping the collective life and imagination of Christian colleges and universities."[10] I believe that the absence of the church as a controlling priority for the Evangelical college is one of the main causes of the secularization

---

7. Gehrz, "'Nothing For Your Journey.'"
8. Gehrz, "'Nothing For Your Journey.'"
9. Johnstone, "Christian Higher Education," 177.
10. Harink, "Taking the University to Church," 396.

that I wish to diagnose. It naturally follows that my modest proposal for reform centers on a recommendation that the Evangelical college reorient its vocation toward the renewal and reformation of the church.

A call for the Evangelical college to organize its vision around the church might appear at first glance to be an attenuated ambition.[11] Many Evangelical colleges have consciously rejected an earlier Bible school paradigm of education that centered on training Christian workers for churchly vocations. Many faculty celebrate liberation from the sometimes stultifying constraints of denominational or ecclesial networks that policed thought and proscribed debate. Elizabeth Newman has noted the way in which "numerous Christian colleges and universities, for the sake of pluralism, have interpreted their own religious tradition as a negative, homogenizing force."[12] Indeed, it was axiomatic for the founding generation of late twentieth-century Christian liberal arts colleges that Evangelical education must leave behind otherworldly pietism and defensive dogmatism and engage more hospitably and sympathetically with culture, the arts, and society at large. "There is, " observes Ronald Kirkemo, "a kind of S-curve that represent the move from one-factor indoctrination through bible-centered education, to education with the plus factor of Christianity, to a modernized liberal arts college that embodies the higher stages of reasoning and analysis."[13] To those who have become accustomed to this way of picturing the evolution of Evangelical colleges my proposal will sound like retrogression to the bad old days of dogmatic religion, third-order moral taboos, and low academic standards.

However, the call for the Evangelical college to embrace an ecclesial vocation only sounds narrow because we lack a robust understanding of the vocation of the church itself. By simultaneously *restricting* our vision of the Evangelical college to focus on its ecclesial vocation and then also *broadening* our vision of the Christian church, a new vision of a more fully Evangelical education may emerge. Far from constraining the vision of the Christian college, the call for it to orient its priorities around strengthening and renewing the church is the most liberating and panoramic option one

11. For example, Ream and Glanzer argue that a holistic Christian education must go beyond "biblical knowledge or vocations within the church." While I know what they are trying to say, this statement also reveals a characteristically pejorative vision of both Bible and church. Ream and Glanzer, *Idea of a Christian College*, 7.

12. Newman, *Divine Abundance*, 26.

13. Ronald Kirkemo, "Point Loma Nazarene College: Modernization in Christian Higher Education," in Hughes and Adrian, eds., *Models*, 349.

could imagine. This is because the calling of the church is exhilaratingly capacious: to join the mission of God in the renewal of all things, and "to live out within the present old order of the world the truths and values of the in-breaking new order of the kingdom of God."[14] As Douglas Harink argues, the church is

> a living icon of what the culture might become . . . were it to allow itself to be re-created by the Gospel . . . The Church is itself called to instantiate a new social existence bringing forth altered social relationships, a new political reality bringing forth transformed political arrangements, a new art form generating new artistic creations, a new university bringing forth un-thought-of intellectual constructions, a new ecology forming new relationships with the earth, stars and animals. The Church is called to become the realization in particular times and places of the reconciliation, resurrection, and renewal of all things (in particular, its host culture) in conformity with Christ.[15]

Compared to this breathtaking vision of our calling to participate in this radical, holistic, ecclesial community, the actual vision and practice of many Evangelical colleges is pallidly unambitious. To quote C. S. Lewis, we are like a "child who wants to go on making mud pies in a slum because he cannot imagine what is meant by the offer of a holiday at the sea. We are far too easily pleased."[16] Or, to quote the words of Arthur Holmes, one of the pioneers of modern Evangelical higher education: "by and large we have not dreamed large enough dreams."[17]

The call for Evangelical higher education to embrace a church-focused mission harkens back to a call made by Nicholas Wolterstorff in an address given at the centenary celebrations of Wheaton College in 1983. In this speech Wolterstorff contended that there had been two stages in the evolution of North American Christian colleges. During the first era Christian colleges understood their mission as nurturing individual piety and promoting personal evangelism. In the second era Christian colleges desired to inculcate a Christian understanding of culture. Wolterstorff predicted that the third stage of the Christian college (which he believed was at that time dawning) would be centered on "the Christian in society." This era,

---

14. Wright, *Mission of God*, 311.
15. Harink, "Taking the University to Church," 396.
16. Lewis, *Weight of Glory*, 26.
17. Holmes, *Idea of a Christian College*, 11.

argued Wolterstorff, should take as its defining objective the preparation of students who could act justly in a globalized world.[18]

Many Evangelical colleges would claim that they have embraced this third stage. The mission statements of CCCU institutions express a hope that their graduates will not only *know something* but also be able to *do something*: to "live out biblical truth";[19] to apply "Christian values";[20] to promote "biblical models of leadership";[21] to "influence our world";[22] to "impact the world";[23] to "impact the world for Jesus";[24] to "advance the cause of Christ";[25] to "make a difference in the world for Jesus";[26] or to "advance the work of God."[27] Just as the constrained, defensive, and narrowly religious first stage of the Christian college was eclipsed by a vision for holistic thinking and a robust commitment to the life of the mind during the second epoch of the Evangelical college, so the sometimes cerebral and philosophically laden vision of the second stage appears to have given way to a more activist and socially engaged vision. The Wolterstorffian third age appears to have dawned.

However, Wolterstorff added an important coda to his vision for this "third stage" of Christian higher education. He argued that it should be the era "not only the Christian in society . . . but the stage of the Christian *in the church* in society." The insertion of this ecclesial clause reflected Wolterstorff's belief that "the most fundamental thing to say about the Christian college is that it is an arm of the body of Christ in the world. It is of and by and for the church . . . [it] exists to equip members of the people of God for their lives as members of that people—a people that exists not for its own sake but for the sake of all humanity and thereby to the glory of God."[28]

When this vital additional element of Wolterstorff's picture of the future of the Christian college is highlighted, it becomes evident that he

---

18. Wolterstorff, *Educating for Shalom*, 33.
19. Bethel University, "Mission."
20. Grace College, "Educational Values."
21. North Central University, "About."
22. Cornerstone University, "Employment."
23. San Diego Christian University, "Why."
24. Montreat College, "Vision."
25. Asbury University, "Foundations."
26. Corban University, "Who We Are."
27. Azusa Pacific University, "At a Glance."
28. Wolterstorff, *Educating for Shalom*, 335.

was a prophet without honor. While many Evangelical colleges want their graduates to live rich, creative, and consequential Christian lives, most portray this as a singular effort of the individual student rather than of the individual living within a Christian community. There is little evidence that Evangelical colleges think that their primary mission is to help students find their place within the church, nor that they aim to help students understand the church as the primary agent of God's mission in the world. Only around one-quarter of CCCU-member institution mission statements make any mention of the church whatsoever.[29] If we take seriously the claim of Glanzer et al. that failing to "mention the church as a sphere where the educated person can use one's knowledge" is a sign of the secularization of a Christian college, then 75 percent of CCCU institutions are secularizing.[30] Of those colleges that do use the word "church" in their mission statements, nearly all list the church only as one of a number of venues—alongside other arenas such as "society," "culture," "professions," and "family"—in which the college hoped individual graduates would serve.[31] This inclusion of the church as one of multiple venues for service does not do justice to the Wolterstorffian notion that the church must provide the overarching rationale and *telos* of the Christian college, nor to his argument that individuals can only serve society in and through the church. Instead, it reflects a voluntarist notion of the church that is dominant in North American society, in which the church is just one of myriad communities to which the individual may choose to belong.

Even Wolterstorff's own Calvin University (an institution with a strong ecclesial connection to the Christian Reformed Church in North America) has, according to two of its eminent professors, James D. Bratt and Ronald A. Wells, "shown little inclination" to move toward the paradigm delineated by Wolterstorff.[32] In fact, thirty years after Wolterstorff's invocation, another notable Calvin scholar, James K. A. Smith, expressed disappointment that Christian colleges failed to cast their mission around priorities shaped by an understanding of the mission of the church. "If something like Christian universities are to exist," argued Smith (with a rhetorical inflexion that hinted that maybe they shouldn't), "they should

---

29. Firmin and Gilson, "Mission Statement Analysis"; Woodrow, "Institutional Image."

30. Glanzer et al., *Restoring the Soul*, 136.

31. This was based on my own survey carried out in 2019.

32. Bratt and Wells, "Piety and Progress," in Hughes and Adrian, eds., *Models*, 159.

be configured as extensions of the mission of the church . . . [They exist] to form radical disciples of Jesus and citizens of the baptismal city who, communally, take up the creational task of being God's image bears, unfolding the cultural possibilities latent in creation—but doing so as empowered by the Spirit, following the example of Jesus' cruciform cultural labor." However, Smith did not think Christian colleges were configured to meet this goal. "To be blunt," he observed, "our Christian colleges and universities generate an army of alumni who look pretty much like all the rest of their suburban neighbors, except that our graduates drive their SUVs, inhabit their executive homes, and pursue the frenetic life of the middle class and the corporate ladder 'from a Christian perspective.'"[33]

The reason for this neglect of the church flows from several interlocking causes. These include: a thin theology of the church among many Evangelical Protestants in general; a gradual loosening of ties between Christian colleges and specific denominations; and the denominational, and even religious, diversity of the student, faculty, and staff body at many Evangelical colleges that naturally tends toward a generic "Christian" identity, devoid of possibly divisive endorsement of a *particular* Christian confessional community, liturgical practice, or distinctive theological principle. However, it might also be argued that talk of the church—a radical, countercultural, sacrificial community—is avoided because orienting the college toward the mission of the church would be incredibly risky and disruptive to an established model of Evangelical higher education which promises to provide students access to the modern economy. As James K. A. Smith has observed: "It is clear that those who support Christian universities would be quite upset if the qualifier [Christian] came to mean that the education students received might put them at a disadvantage for being a success in America."[34]

The absence of the church in the imagination and actions of Evangelical colleges has a corollary: the absence of the Evangelical college as a meaningful force within the church, and particularly within those churches marked by the dominant characteristics of Evangelicalism. Since Evangelical colleges do not orient their mission around the renewal of the church, the church does not generally engage with Evangelical teachers and scholars. Christian academics often lament the lack of engagement between the Christian academy and the church. However, this critique is often framed

---

33. Smith, *Desiring the Kingdom*, 218–19.
34. Smith, *Desiring the Kingdom*, 223.

in terms of the failure of Christian *scholars* to reach the church.³⁵ The failure of Christian scholarship to trickle into the sanctuary may indeed be a cause for lament, but I think the more regrettable phenomenon is the failure of the Christian *college* to reach the people of God. This latter failure is tragic because, while lone scholars might understandably find it hard to gain a hearing within Christian communities, the church itself *turns up at the gates of the Evangelical college* every year, in the form of approximately half a million students currently enrolled in CCCU institutions. The Evangelical college is uniquely positioned to summon, nurture, catechize, and renew the Evangelical community, and yet, as I will attempt to show in the remainder of this book, it often squanders the opportunity. This is a scandal.

Many readers will realize that this talk of "scandal" is a parody of Mark Noll's influential book *The Scandal of the Evangelical Mind*, first published in 1989. In this work Noll damned the anti-intellectualism that he argued pervades the American Evangelical community. While Noll attributed this phenomenon to numerous historical factors, he laid some of the blame at the door of the Christian college which, he concluded, can only ever "provide general guidance, general orientation, and general introduction." Christian colleges, he opined "were created for specifically religious purposes," and thus "were not designed to promote thorough Christian reflection on the nature of the world, society, and the arts . . . It is little wonder they miss so badly that for which they do not aim."³⁶ In making this critique Noll was thinking primarily of whether undergraduate teaching-focused colleges could promote a coherent body of Christian thought and Christian scholarship. He was probably right to argue that they cannot—at least, not as their primary outcome. However, as *The Scandal of the Evangelical Mind* made clear, the problem with Evangelicalism in North America has not simply been an absence of Evangelical scholars at work in the academy. Rather it has been the demotic, populist, and culturally bound ethos of the Evangelical movement in the pews.

On this point Noll was, I believe, unnecessarily dismissive of the *potential* of the Evangelical college to address this broader malaise of Evangelicalism. Because his vision was oriented around Christian thinkers and Christian scholarship, he damned Christian colleges for offering only survey classes. Yet this conclusion underestimated how much "even" a general survey class might radically deepen an average Evangelical student's

---

35. Green, "On the Evangelical Mind," 338.
36. Noll, *Scandal* (1989), 16.

The Scandal Identified

understanding of the world, especially if she or he has hitherto lived only in the narrow and sometimes dogmatically constrained sphere of church, home, Christian school, and the social media echo chamber. Indeed the very factors that Noll saw as undermining the cultivation of Evangelical scholarship on the campus of Christian colleges—namely, that they attract students of variable academic qualities, that they are intended to serve religious constituencies, that they prioritize generalized over specialist knowledge, that they value praxis as much as abstract thinking, and that they ask their professors to invest heavily in teaching—could be reinterpreted as the vital factors that provide Christian colleges with a unique opportunity to educate ordinary Evangelicals. This is not to say that Evangelical colleges *are* doing this—the gist of what I will argue in the rest of the book is that they are *not*—merely that there is a latent potential for the Evangelical college that does not reside in its cultivation of Evangelical thinkers.

These observations mean that the scandal I want to describe is not the same as that diagnosed by Noll. I do not intend to lament the paucity of Evangelical scholarship or the poverty of the Evangelical "mind." In fact, Noll himself has acknowledged that there are today plenty of Evangelical scholars, some of whom are faculty at Evangelical colleges. As historian Jay Green observes: "If [Noll's] book aimed to energize a generation of evangelicals to establish themselves in elite universities, to produce credible, meaningful scholarship, and to leave a record of thoughtful reflection on modern culture, then mission accomplished!"[37] This fact, however, has not solved the problem. As Joel Carpenter has ruminated: "What good did it do for Mark Noll to receive a medal from a U.S. president for his virtuous achievements, when evangelical voters in two successive elections overwhelmingly supported an amoral and dangerous presidential candidate who was profoundly lacking in the virtues needed to serve in high office?"[38] Indeed, Noll himself has pondered why the renaissance of Evangelical scholarship that has occurred since he first wrote *Scandal* has failed to make a difference to a Evangelical church in which "no half-baked conspiracy, however lacking in responsible verification, seems too much.

---

37. Green, "On the Evangelical Mind." For a contrary opinion that "the scandal Mark Noll astutely brought into view remains plenty evident in the CCCU," see Miller, "Anti-Intellectualism."

38. Carpenter, "Reawakening Evangelical Intellectual Life."

Are the Christian colleges and universities failing; or are they just spitting into the whirlwind?"[39]

The reason for the malaise is that the issue was never simply *anti-intellectualism*—at least, not an anti-intellectualism that can be cured by increasing the number of Christian scholars. Rather, the scandal of American Evangelicalism is a holistic scandal of Evangelical *identity*, or what Mark Labberton has called simply "the crisis of Evangelicalism."[40] By this is meant the way in which much of ethnically Anglophone European American "White" Evangelicalism has become captive to a set of powerful cultural ideologies that set them apart both from historic Christianity (including previous generations of Evangelicals) and from much of the global Evangelical community.[41] It is not simply the case that Evangelicals are hostile to the mind; many Evangelicals are scandalously inert to *the evangel and* have wrapped it in a bundle of sociocultural and political assumptions. As Thomas S. Kidd, a prominent historian of Evangelicalism, observed in 2020: "I believe that something has gone terribly wrong in much of white evangelical culture, though I remain as committed as ever to historic evangelical beliefs and practices."[42] Large swathes of American Evangelicalism has become, just like its colleges, scandalously secularized.

Ensuring that Evangelicals are witnessing faithfully to the good news of Jesus Christ is therefore vital and urgent work in calling back the Evangelical community to the *evangel*. Evangelical colleges are in a unique position to attend to this mission. Like the local church, they interface with a substantial body of local Evangelical Christians, but, unlike the local

---

39. Noll, *Scandal* (2022), xi.

40. Labberton, "Political Dealing."

41. I have both capitalized, and placed quotation marks around, the term "White" to convey, no doubt imperfectly, both that racial categories are invented, and that the term "White" is a legal and social label that has been historically applied to certain persons in the United States based on a combination of their European ancestry, skin color, legal status, self-identity, and social authentication. It is a term that, like other racial labels, hovers between being an historical fiction (hence enclosing it in ironic scare quotes) and a sociological and legal reality (hence the capitalization). The use of the term is merely descriptive of a discernable set of predilections that exist within a certain social-ethnic-religious group in the United States. The usage of the color-coded label does not, of course, imply that mere skin color or any other actual or imagined physical quality of an individual is either a predictor or cause of individual or collectiuve attitudes or actions, an idea which, if believed, would validate the very faulty premises of racial categorization that gave us the term to begin with.

42. Kidd, *Who Is An Evangelical?*, 3.

The Scandal Identified

church, they possess the skill, time, and energy to devote to introducing Evangelicals to deeper, more nuanced ways of thinking about the world, themselves, and their Christian identity and vocation. And yet Evangelical colleges do not take the education of the Evangelical community to be their primary *raison d'etre*. They do not orient their priorities, curriculum, and controlling paradigms around the pressing needs of the American Evangelical ecclesial network. Rather they tend to view Evangelical Christian identity as a given; a stable, uncontestable, unproblematic entity—sometimes branded as "the Christian worldview" or "a Christian perspective" or simply as "faith"—which is then injected, infused or "integrated" into the educational enterprise. This *sounds* like it is making Christian faith and practice important: we teach you this, that, and the other, but we do so from a Christian perspective! In fact, by making *this, that, and the other* the *object* of the sentence, Christ is in danger of being relegated to an adjectival qualifier. Evangelical colleges, and the voluminous writing on Evangelical education, therefore often "assume[s] that education has a pre-established form, and the arguments focus upon whether this form or that can be Christianized."[43] I will argue that by importing a pre-existing framework of higher education into the Evangelical college and then trying to sacralize it, Evangelical colleges in fact often invite the opposite: the secularization of Christianity. They thus not only squander a vital opportunity to serve the church; they also, albeit from the best of intentions, inadvertently distort and fracture the *evangel*.

My charge that Evangelical colleges are secularized institutions is made with conscious irony since many Evangelical colleges possess a heritage shaped by a defensive spirit that deliberately and proudly resisted secularization. The liberalization of historic Christian denominations and colleges in the late-nineteenth and early twentieth centuries has generated an enduring perception that Christian colleges should be on their guard against the corrosive effects of modern academic presumptions. Historical accounts of American higher education by George Marsden and James Tunstead Burtchaell have demonstrated the ways in which many American colleges founded on religious principles lost their first love when they embraced modern scholarship and liberal conceptualizations of civilization, reason, and progress. This development represented a tragic "dying of the

---

43. Robert W. Brimlow, "Who Invited Mammon?," in Budde and Wright, eds., *Conflicting Allegiances*, 162.

light" in North American higher education.⁴⁴ By contrast, Evangelical colleges have typically perceived themselves to be institutions committed to keeping the faith. They have imagined themselves as shielded from those howling gales of modernist thinking and decadent morality that have corroded other formerly faith-based institutions.

Although many Evangelical colleges have broadened their theological and intellectual vision since their earlier reactionary or "fundamentalist" days, a desire to maintain an essential, countercultural piety and faith is still a powerful mentality in the Evangelical college. There remains a widespread lurking fear that Evangelical colleges might, if they drop their guard, fall prey to the same secularizing forces that corroded the faith of other once-pious institutions. "Stentorian exhortations against slipping down the slope to secularism have long echoed across CCCU campuses."⁴⁵ Such fears about secularization include the concern that colleges will capitulate to evolution, take a looser view of the authority and reliability of Scripture, embrace moral and epistemological relativism, adopt fashionable ideologies that are perceived to be inimical to Christian orthodoxy, or that individual faculty will empty their scholarly endeavors of anything explicitly Christian to gain a hearing in the profession at large and succumb to the presumed moral and religious vacuity of the rootless academy and naked public square.

However, my accusation that the Evangelical college has secularized has little to do with these classic marks of secularization. While it is possible to find some theologically conservative commentators who lament that the Christian colleges today are more liberal than the Bible schools or fundamentalist colleges of yore, a large body of evidence suggests that many Evangelical colleges have generally *not* succumbed to doctrinal laxity or theological compromise.⁴⁶ For example, if one reviews the list of secularizing tendencies enumerated by William Ringenberg—including institutions abandoning chapel requirements, dropping mission statements

---

44. Marsden and Longfield, eds., *Secularization of the Academy*; Burtchaell, *Dying of the Light*. See also Ringenberg, *Christian College*, and Carpenter and Shipps, eds., *Making Higher Education Christian*.

45. George M. Marsden, "Moving Up the Slippery Slope," in Joeckel and Chesnes, eds., *Christian College Phenomenon*, 333.

46. For example, blogger Tim Bayly calls what he perceives to be moral and doctrinal laxity in the "scandal" of the Evangelical college. Bayly, "Scandal." Laats notes similar concerns voiced by B. Myron Cedarholm of Marantha Baptist Bible College, Wisconsin, who observed that "all across this nation heresy has occurred at Northfield, Providence, Wheaton, Biola, Westmont, Fuller, Denver Seminary etc." Laats, *Fundamentalist U*, 209.

The Scandal Identified

about centrality of Christ, and eliminating hiring policies that ask faculty to affirm vital faith statements—then CCCU colleges are positioned well away from the classic secularization danger zone. The termination of Wheaton College political science professor Larycia Hawkins over controversial views about whether Muslims worship the same God as Christians seem to suggest that administrations are still very keen to police the "orthodox" borders of their campuses.[47] Reviewing responses to a survey administered to faculty at thirty-seven CCCU schools, Samuel Joeckel and Thomas Chesnes concluded that "though vigilance should still be exercised, these institutions are hardly descending the slippery slope to secularization."[48]

In fact, no less a figure than George Marsden has affirmed that Evangelical colleges are unlikely to secularize. Nervous that his work describing the historical secularization of the American university had created paranoia among Evangelical educators about their own potential de-sacralization, Marsden wanted "to set the record straight" by asserting that "an imminent peril of a slide into apostasy and secularism does not describe the current position of the great majority of CCCU schools . . . CCCU schools have histories over the past century that are in some relevant ways almost the opposite of histories of most mainline Protestant colleges and universities."[49]

This evidence might make my claim that Evangelical colleges are secularized institutions seem off-target. If George Marsden is for us, then who can be against us? However, two points need to be made. First, there is more than one way down the slippery slope of secularization; or perhaps we should say there is more than one slippery slope of secularization. Focusing on the classic twentieth-century secularization symptoms manifested by religious institutions—scientific naturalism, religious pluralism, atheistic evolution, higher critical approaches to the Bible, moral relativism, and an erosion of vital faith among faculty and administration—and concluding that, overall, none of this applies to the modern Evangelical college is an attitude dangerously blind to other ways in which a Christian institution might secularize. It is true enough that Evangelical colleges have not traded faith for intellectual respectability, nor sacrificed zeal for obeisance to the pluralistic, relativistic, materialistic (or whatever your choice of *plat de*

---

47. Smietana, "Wheaton College Suspends."

48. Samuel Joeckel and Thomas Chesnes, "A Slippery Slope to Secularization," in Joeckel and Chesnes, eds., *Christian College Phenomenon*, 37.

49. Marsden, "Moving Up," in Joeckel and Chesnes, eds., *Christian College Phenomenon*, 329–33. See also Marsden, *Soul of the American University*, 365–90.

The Scandal of the Evangelical College

jour anti-Christian ideologies) presumed to be at work in the "secular" or "mainstream" academy or society at large. The Evangelical college has not moved to Athens. But it is an unwarranted assumption that it is therefore still in Jerusalem.

Second, emphasizing the high degrees of religiosity on campus overlooks the fact that the religious subculture (i.e., White American Evangelicalism), which is perceived to be proof the *absence* of secularization on campus, might itself be a carrier of deeply secular assumptions. High levels of Evangelical zeal and rhetoric in the Evangelical college are not enough to prove that the college is not secularized *if the Evangelical tradition itself is already afflicted by secularity*. In seeking to defend against intellectual liberalization, Evangelical colleges import the very peculiar religious, ethnic, political, and ideological traits of American Evangelicalism that they ought to be challenging. They are not (to borrow Noll's phrase) "spitting into the whirlwind" of Evangelical malaise; they are institutionalizing the storm.

These two observations form the framework for the remainder of this book. In chapter 2 I will argue that there is little truly Christian about the overarching purpose and patterns of education in most Evangelical colleges. Programs are added and subtracted based on the need to recruit students by promising them ready access to jobs in the American market economy, not because of any particular theological first principle about what is needed to equip the people of God for the mission of God. In chapter 3, I will argue that this reality means that many attempts by professors to link Christianity to the subjects taught at Evangelical colleges will inevitably create tangential or banal "connections" with Christianity because the pedagogical project is driven by the priorities of disciplinary or professional knowledge rather than by the narrative arc or theological imperatives of Christianity.

The fact that most Evangelical colleges look very similar to other educational institutions—and are becoming more so as they race to provide cheaper, shorter, more market-sensitive degrees—means that greater emphasis must be placed on the "spiritual" climate of campus as proof the "Christian" credentials. This is theme of chapter 4. Colleges assert their Evangelical *bona fides* in cocurricular activities such as chapel, and in public rhetorical postures. In seeking to recruit students from a polarized political culture, colleges often embrace ideologies that appeal to the White Evangelical constituency from which they receive donations and support. While generally insouciant about what goes on in the classroom, administrators are ready to pounce if faculty trip the wires of the invisible cultural-political tests of American Evangelical orthodoxy. Evangelical colleges thus lack the critical distance or moral capacity to address the scandal of Evangelicalism. They see Evangelical Christianity as that which solves the problem of education, rather than education as that which might address the scandal of Evangelicalism.

Chapter 5 proposes a remedy: a reimagination of the relationship between faith and learning as a project that is centered on the urgent task of bringing spiritual, ethical, and evangelical renewal to the Evangelical Christian community. Unlike the typical presidential or board vision premised on growth—more students, more buildings, more programs, which all too often require diminution of both academic quality and Christian distinctives alongside large budgetary outlays—this proposal might create a much more affordable Christian college, while increasing both academic depth *and* Christian distinctives.

Despite the Goldilocks temper of the previous sentence, this book is not written under any illusion that it will trigger a seismic reformation of the sector, nor that it will convince readers who have never experienced the dull aches of disquietude concerning the current state of Evangelical higher education. Indeed, in one sense it is not written to *convince* anyone at all. As many writers will attest, the primary reason for writing a book is to explain things to oneself; to distill, organize, and even justify to oneself the bundle of inchoate feelings, ideas, and analytical fragments that accumulate in one's mind and emotions over time. If this book has a purpose beyond personal catharsis, it is to help others identify and decipher their own nagging thoughts and anxieties about Christian education. To these readers I hope the following pages might give encouragement that you are not alone, reassurance that your feelings are not without reason, and courage to find a voice and imagine a different future.

Chapter 2

Christ and the Catalog

"ONE CAN TELL MUCH about the religious orientation of a college by carefully examining its catalog," argues William Ringenberg.[1] Let us follow his advice. To understand just how undistinctive the Evangelical college is, all one needs to do is flip through an average Evangelical college academic catalog. Listed therein is a suite of majors and minors virtually indistinguishable from any nonreligious institution. Some of these programs have been inherited from the classical vision of liberal arts and social sciences. Many others have been added in the last three decades in response to the growing demand for professional and STEM qualifications. The Evangelical college divides its programs along typical disciplinary and vocational lines, and its classes fulfill the usual requirements of a major or minor program in that subject area, not least to ensure transferability and professional accreditation.

James Woodrow has argued that "most colleges and universities prefer to mirror the culture they serve. In an age of secularism, though, Christ-centered institutions continuously challenge the culture and its prevailing values."[2] Such self-congratulatory statements pepper the literature on Evangelical education. But are they true? Regarding the suite of programs on offer at most Evangelical colleges, the catalog is clearly a mirror image of

---

1. Ringenberg, *Christian College*, 121. Ringenberg proceeded to review several Christian college catalogs and adjudged them still Christian. However, he looked only at the *statement of belief* printed *in* the catalog, not the bulk of the catalog itself. In this chapter I intend to take his advice more literally than he himself did!

2. James Woodrow, "Institutional Image," in Joeckel and Chesnes, *Christian College Phenomenon*, 315.

those secular universities that, according to Woodrow, mirror the culture that they serve! This point has not been lost on critics of Evangelical colleges. Adam Laats, a self-styled "outsider" to the Evangelical college phenomenon, observed, "when we look at what evangelicals have done with their interdenominational colleges . . . we are struck immediately by the fact that they are overwhelmingly more similar than different from the rest of America."[3] Christian educator Ronald Kirkemo even celebrates the Christian college hitting a sweet-spot identity in harmony with the "cosmopolitan and open-minded mainstream of American culture."[4]

One response to my accusation that Evangelical colleges look very similar to non-Evangelical colleges might be to point out that the distinction claimed by an Evangelical college is not that they teach *different subjects* than other institutions, but rather that they teach the same subjects *differently*. Most apologists for Evangelical education would agree with Patrick Allen and Kenneth Badley when they claim that Christian colleges "want to help students understand their studies in a fundamentally different way than do students who complete the same major or program in a college that does not claim Christ."[5] Indeed George Marsden has argued that it is precisely this commitment to hiring faculty who will "engage in the integration of faith and learning" that will preserve Evangelical colleges from tumbling into the secular abyss. "CCCU schools have built a sense of difference into the very fabric of the academic enterprise," he asserts.[6]

I will address this claim about "teaching Christianly" directly in the next chapter. Suffice it here to say that I do not think that this necessarily preserves the Evangelical college from secularity. Paradoxically, it may precipitate it. However, even if the claim that Evangelical colleges teach the same subjects differently *is* a valid defense against my argument, I believe it is only a defense at the level of individual classes and for individual professors. At this juncture, however, I want to press home the argument that the *full catalog* is a powerful statement that deserves consideration on its own terms. It is the document that puts into concrete terms what the institution wants to do. We are therefore entitled to ask whether the *curriculum itself* arises from a Christian perspective or, indeed, whether it is directed toward

---

3. Laats, *Fundamentalist U*, 79.
4. Kirkemo, "Point Loma," in Hughes and Adrian, eds., *Models*. 349.
5. Allen and Badley, *Faith and Learning*, 37.
6. Marsden, "Moving Up," in Joeckel and Chesnes, eds., *Christian College Phenomenon*, 333.

a Christian end. If an institution is said to be Christ-centered, surely Christ should be at the center not only of each individual class, but also he in whom all the catalog holds together.

We can make the question more specific: do administrators add or eliminate programs according to any discernible theological or missiological principle? If they do, I am not sure it has ever been revealed in the voluminous literature on the integration of faith and learning. Indeed, Perry Glanzer and Todd Ream have noted that "we continually find it amazing that some presidents, provosts, and administrators at some Christian universities have . . . not read widely about what it means to lead a Christian university in this area [of the integration of faith and learning]."[7] This is astounding. In reality, as I suspect most faculty know, the contours of the academic curriculum of the Evangelical college are not set by Christianity at all, but by a presumption about student appetite for certain programs, which are in turn shaped by the demands of the job market, and refracted through analysis of what peer institutions (secular and sacred) are offering. They are subject to SWOT analysis, studies of market opportunity, and revenue streams. In all this, Evangelical colleges are in reality "more market driven than mission driven."[8]

This Christian market pragmatism is exemplified in a survey of graphic design courses at Christian colleges undertaken by Lorraine Bower. When asked if he had a set of guiding principles that he used for developing curriculum one respondent to the survey replied: "Not really . . . because on one level I know that this is what the student needs to get a job." Meanwhile a college principal "described the rationale for the development of the graphic design course out of the visual arts course. 'More people wanted to do it,' he said, and 'it was more practical; students could get jobs.'" As Bower concluded: "In contrast to their religious mission, graphic design courses are sometimes introduced in Protestant evangelical institutions for largely practical reasons."[9]

---

7. Glanzer et al., *Restoring the Soul*, 237.

8. Susie C. Stanley and John E. Stanley, "What can the Wesleyan/Holiness tradition contribute to Christian higher education," in Hughes and Adrian, eds., *Models for Christian Higher Education*, 325. The authors were referring to Wesleyan/Holiness schools but there seems no reason to limit the observation. See also Paul Toews, "Religious Idealism," in Hughes and Adrian, eds., *Models*, 236; Jacobsen "History and Character," in Hughes and Adrian, eds., *Models*, 341.

9. Bower, "Faith-Learning," 8–9.

This is not some unique quirk of graphic design programs. One could extend this conclusion to *most* subjects on offer at the Evangelical college campus. Indeed, the regnant cultural ambience of the Evangelical college is pragmatism and market sensitivity. As Marie S. Morris admits, "economic, technological, and global challenges . . . result in a formidable competition, not unlike a battlefield. With declining endowments, donors' waning confidence in their ability to carry through with pledged funds, cuts to federal and state financial aid, and families demanding affordability, a greater focus on efficiency is required as institutions engage the battle for limited resources."[10] Dawn Tolbert argues that Christian colleges have not only adopted marketing terminology in the realm of publicity and recruitment but also have allowed the marketing culture to reshape how the institutions view and interact with students, alumni, and other constituent groups.[11] In other words, what began as pragmatic response to publicize the institution starts to seep into the overall ethos of the institution to form a deep "liturgy"—to use Jamie K. A. Smith's term—that pervades the entire institution. Messiah College history professor John Fea observed this phenomenon when his daughter toured several Evangelical colleges: "My daughter . . . realized that admission officers knew how to sell programs but did not know how to talk about an education at a Christian college in a way that transcended utilitarian ends."[12]

Off the record, some Christian college provosts and presidents admit this reality. Conversations undertaken by Perry Glanzer and Todd Ream with ten senior Evangelical college leaders revealed that the Christian university is "both complicit in fueling student careerism and consumerism, and that, perhaps worse yet, it has taken to modeling that behavior for students." One provost noted that "we're in so deep in the system and the system is deep in another system it's hard to figure out what can be done." "Is it too late for Christian higher education to be a credible critic of the very system of which we are so complicit?" asked another.[13] Such questions ought to be widely discussed and candidly debated among all CCCU member institutions. If senior administrators admit such things in private, aren't they somewhat disingenuous when they promote platitudes about

---

10. Marie S. Morris, "Metaphors Matter: Organizational Culture Shaped By Image," in Longman, *Thriving in Leadership*, 108.
11. Tolbert, "An Exploration."
12. Fea, "State of the Evangelical Mind."
13. Glanzer et al., *Restoring the Soul*, 302–5.

Christ-centered education? And aren't faculty being naïvely utopian when they formulate their high-minded philosophies of Christian education that, while they can be beautiful and compelling, are often blind to the really existing Evangelical college in which they will have to be implemented?

While administrators might wring their hands and claim that economic survival necessitates a compromise of high-minded principles, it should be noted that the Evangelical college has not simply the victim of external forces beyond her control. Adam Laats notes that colleges founded as Fundamentalist bastions against the rising tide of secularism paradoxically "accepted without much fuss other elements of the modern academic revolution. For example . . . just like mainstream [colleges, they] simply assumed as the twentieth century progressed that their role was to prepare students for specific professions."[14] Similarly, in his discussion of Azusa Pacific University James Burtchaell noted that "it has been Azusa not the WASC [Western Association of Schools and Colleges] that tended repeatedly to construe Christian faith in terms that appealed to a wider clientele but thinned its substance."[15] In a similar vein, Elizabeth Newman has observed that "as Christian colleges have embraced normative pluralism, their allegiance has shifted unsurprisingly from the church to the guild and the nation."[16] Here we reach the nub of the broadest level of secularization at work in the Evangelical college. As Martin Marty has observed: "If our schools are 'secularizing,' they are doing so not because a secular humanist conspiracy or a group of Supreme Court or theologically liberal subversives are leading in that direction. They are doing so unthinkingly, by adopting the material norms of a market economy."[17] Eschewing both Athens *and* Jerusalem, the Evangelical college has relocated to Tyre and Sidon.

The regnant secularized culture that prevails on the Evangelical campus means that Christian professors will generally find themselves to be prophets without honor if they ask whether the Evangelical college has any business adding this or that program, or if they seek to resist the dictates of market sensitivity and financial exigency as the basis for decision-making. Who would dare to utter Robert Brimlow's provocative question, "who invited Mammon?" and inquire as to what business Christian colleges have in

---

14. Laats, *Fundamentalist U*, 25–26.
15. Burtchaell, *Dying of the Light*, 772.
16. Newman, *Divine Abundance*, 26.
17. Marty, "Church and Christian Higher Education in the New Millennium," in Agee and Henry, eds., *Faithful Learning*, 54.

offering degrees in business and finance?[18] These departments often generate the most revenue for the Evangelical college. It would seem absurd to question them. Yet this means that while many have feared that Christian colleges restrict academic freedom because of their faith commitments, it is possible that the bigger problem is that Evangelical colleges restrict *Christian* freedom—the freedom to dissent from the overarching protocols, assumptions, and priorities of the modern American political economy—because of their prevailing secular assumptions.[19] As Samuel Zalanga has argued (using the word "Pietist" here to refer to colleges in the formal "Pietist" tradition, although in an observation that applies to all "Evangelical" institutions): "Today there is a need for a bold commitment to the struggle for justice . . . Unfortunately contemporary universities and colleges in the Pietist tradition cannot faithfully do so because they would be perceived as anti-American, socialist and anticapitalist. Such charges would drain away institutional social capital and financial support, and draw negative publicity."[20]

Given the utilitarian nature of overarching programmatic decisions, the mandate of the individual faculty member to "integrate faith and learning" (or some similar construal of linking Christianity with the programs of the institution) is based on shakier ground than is often admitted. After all, if a program itself has not been added based on discernible, theological, ecclesial, or missiological grounds, then there is no inherent basis for believing that we can teach it "from a Christian perspective," nor that it necessarily helps advance whichever model of Christian formation or "kingdom impact" to which the college aspires. After all, what if the correct "Christian perspective" on a particular program or suite of classes within a program is that *there is nothing particularly, distinctly, or uniquely Christian about this subject?* Or even—whisper it!—what if the "Christian perspective" is actually that *Christians should not be taking part in the activities or conforming themselves to the protocols required by this kind of program or professional training?* The Evangelical college cannot allow itself to ask such questions.

Instead, once a decision has been made on pragmatic grounds to run a program the Evangelical college *is compelled* to construct a Christian

---

18. Brimlow, "Who Invited Mammon?" in Budde and Wright, eds., *Conflicting Allegiances*.

19. Yoder, "Classroom Advocacy," 95.

20. Samuel Zalinga, "Neoliberal Challenges to the Pietist Vision of Christian Higher Education," in Gehrz, ed., *Pietist Vision*, 219.

apologia for it. The result is not actually a Christ-centered university at all, but a college in which Christ offers an alibi for the existence of basically secular, market-driven programs. Crucially, as I will explain further in the next chapter, the attempt at "integrating" faith into an essentially secular set of disciplines will always *secularize* Christianity, since it will make the Bible bow to the discipline or professional program and forces the Bible to yield up often tenuous or incidental insights determined not by the scriptural narrative but rather by the content of a class or program. The Evangelical college thus entices its faculty to paint a "veneer of biblicism" over the secular subjects it has decided to employ them to teach.[21] Of course, some faculty do better than this, but when they do so it is often in spite of, not because of, the overarching circumstances in which they are asked to work.

KUYPER AND FRIENDS

An interlocutor might argue that I am asking too much by demanding that the Evangelical college justify individual programs or classes on theological or missiological grounds since there is a broader paradigm within which the Evangelical college operates that legitimizes a broad multidisciplinary catalog. The basic assumption of such a paradigm is that the world is not divided between "sacred" and "secular" zones and that the Christians are therefore authorized to learn about and work within multiple arenas of life. A neat summary of the outlook is provided by John C. Stevens of Abilene University, who states that because they whole universe belongs to God, "there are no subjects on this earth, or in outer space, or in the metaphysical realm, which we cannot study on the campus of a Christian institution."[22] This is a serious counterargument to my damnatory clauses. It deserves to be scrutinized in depth.

There are actually three specific theories mobilized to support the type of claim exemplified by Stevens. They are sometimes elided although they possess significant differences from each other when studied in their pure form. The first perspective is associated with the Dutch politician and Christian thinker Abraham Kuyper. Kuyper wrote that "there is not a square inch in the whole domain of our human existence over which Christ, who

---

21. Rampersad, "Meaning," 36.
22. Barnard, "Faith and Campus Culture," in Joeckel and Chesnes, eds., *Christian College Phenomenon*, 108.

is Sovereign over all, does *not* cry, Mine!"[23] The second concept is the notion associated with American theologian H. Richard Niebuhr, who argued that the most appropriate way to understand the relationship of God (and by extension, it is often implied, the Christian church) to society is neither hostility nor acquiescence but "transformation." This insight is often assumed to mean that if Christ transforms culture, then Christians should also transform culture, which must necessitate a broad-based engagement with all sectors of human existence. The third idea is of older pedigree. It stretches back to Augustine of Hippo and other early church fathers. In the context of modern Evangelical education, it was given salience by Frank E. Gaebelein and Arthur Holmes. This is the notion that "All Truth is God's Truth."[24] This assertion implies that the search for truth cannot be narrowly limited to Scripture or putatively "Christian" texts but must lead to multifaceted studies of all areas of reality in search for insights into the creator.

Taken together, these three concepts are powerful affirmations of God's comprehensive sovereignty over all things. They protest any vision of reality that restricts God to a merely sacred, spiritual, ethereal, or interior sphere of existence. However, I do not believe any of these justify much of what goes on in Evangelical colleges today. They are often invoked casually, and the full import of their respective visions is rarely implemented at any kind of institution-wide level. To demonstrate this contention, I will examine each concept in turn.

The Lord of Square Inches

First, we can consider Abraham Kuyper. George Marsden has referred to "the triumph" of Kuyperian thought in Evangelical colleges. This might be overstating the case a little, but there is no doubt that a broadly Kuyperian flavor pervades much of the writing and ruminating about the value, distinctiveness, and methodology of Evangelical higher education. This is true even outside of Reformed circles. For example, the Arminian Northwest Nazarene College hopes that "at the end of their NNU education, we want our students to be able to hear echoes of Abraham Kuyper."[25] Kuyper's insistence that Jesus asserts lordship over every square inch of reality has been useful to Evangelical colleges and academics wishing to distance themselves

---

23. Kuyper, "Sphere Sovereignty," 26.
24. Beck, "All Truth."
25. Northwest Nazarene University, "Crossing the Bridge."

from the kind of anti-intellectualism described by Mark Noll as inherent to the Evangelical tradition. To those who might claim we should focus on saving souls, not learning about philosophy or social work, Kuyper reminds us that Jesus is Lord over all!

Of course, if Kuyperanism simply means that everything belongs to Christ, there can be little dissent. As a protest against dualism, quasi-Gnosticism, and nebulous otherworldly piety Kuyper's most famous dictum is unassailable. However, I am dubious that this basic theological assertion gives *carte blanche* for the Evangelical college to adopt the range of programs that one encounters in their catalogs today. Every square inch belongs to Jesus, but acres of the world disobey and rebel against his sovereign claims.[26] Indeed, the belief that Christ is Lord of all might lead one to embrace the opposite claim, namely that one ought to *challenge* the occupants of the land in the name of the true sovereign, not train students to conform to the protocols of the rebels. Kuyper himself spoke of a cosmic spiritual struggle between the kingdom of light and darkness that "runs through every department of human life and culture, including philosophy and the academic enterprise as a whole, and through the heart of every believer as he struggles to live a life of undivided allegiance to God."[27]

Kuyper's "square inch" assertion makes a grand theological point about the sovereignty of God, but it really tells us nothing about what an Evangelical college should or should not be doing in terms of its programmatic priorities. After all, Christ is sovereign over the square acres of American weed farms. Does that mean we mean we should start a Christ-centered major in marijuana studies? Asserting that Christ is Lord over all is not actually enough when it comes to thinking about education. There must presumably be some other theological form of discernment about what actions are *good* and *right* for people who wish to acknowledge such divine Lordship.

Indeed, it is notable that Kuyper's aphorism is often misquoted as asserting that there is not a square inch "in the whole of *creation*" over which Christ does not claim Lordship. The authentic quote is "in the whole domain of our *human existence*..."[28] The difference is subtle but significant. Kuyper was issuing a *summons* for every aspect of human existence *to respond* to the claims of Christ's sovereignty. It was, in many ways, a call for repentance

---

26. Carson, *Christ and Culture*, 214.
27. Bartholomew, *Contours*, 108.
28. Henderson, "Kuyper's Inch," 12.

in all areas of life—a call to bring everything into conformity with Christ. By contrast, while saying Christ is sovereign over creation is, of course, on the one hand perfectly orthodox, when such a statement is deployed to justify a bundle of academic programs it can turn into a subtle sacralization of that which already exists. The call to repentance is thereby elided in favor of a Jesus who puts his Lordly imprimatur on what we have already decided to do. As (self-confessed Kuyperian) James Bratt complains: "Here's my beef. In announcing that any work can be God's work, we run the risk of saying that any work is God's work. That whatever we want to do, we may do and put a God stamp on it. Wherever, however, with whomever, with all the standard rewards in that field."[29]

Of course, Kuyper himself had more to say than his quotable "square inch" aphorism. He argued that reality consisted of distinct pillars, or spheres, which should operate according to their Christ-given norms. He contended that these spheres do not become Christian when Christians enter them; rather they are *already* under the Lordship of Christ. It was in the context of this argument that Kuyper made his "square inch" claim, his point being that all domains of human existence are already under Christ's dominion and should operate in ways appropriate to their God-given *telos*. Kuyper's insistence on these multiple spheres might again be seen as a refutation of my critique of the "secular" catalog. This is because several of Kuyper's spheres are, at first glance, ostensibly "secular." To anyone catechized in Christian dualism—the kind of sentiment exemplified by the old Gospel song "the world is not my home / I'm just a-passing through"—then "Kuyper opened the whole world for Christian participation."[30] Kuyper insisted on the divinely bestowed dignity of multiple arenas of human existence and demanded "believers . . . extend the logic of their faith to sites they had heretofore ignored."[31] In regard to the Christian college, then, "not just theology and philosophy but *all the academic* disciplines—being but reflection upon the different domains of creation—are part of *Christian education*."[32] It would seem that Kuyper might bless the catalog that I damn.

But there are problems with reaching this conclusion. The average Evangelical college catalog does not match up to the spheres or pillars

29. Bratt, "Why I'm Sick."
30. Bratt and Wells, "Piety and Progress," in Hughes and Adrian, eds., *Models*, 143.
31. Bratt and Noll, *Abraham Kuyper*, 208.
32. Bratt, "What can the Reformed tradition contribute to Christian higher education?" in Hughes and Adrian, eds., *Models*, 138.

enumerated by Kuyper. First, "we must . . . keep in mind, that Kuyper did not proclaim all and sundry to be spheres."[33] He did not talk about a sphere of cyber-security, a sphere of accountancy, or a sphere of sports management. Indeed, it would be quite wrong to equate Kuyper's "spheres" in any simple way with the kind of disciplines or professional programs studied at college, or with the division of the labor force in the modern global economic order. His "spheres" are *not* discrete professional or associational networks, but layers of existence—moral, natural, family, metaphysical, religious, personal, logical, and so on. He thus delineated

> the domain of nature . . . a domain of the personal, of the domestic, of the scientific, of the social, and of the ecclesiastical life; each of which obeys its own law of life, and each subject to its own head. There is a domain of thought in which no law may prevail except the law of logic. A domain of conscience where none may exercise sovereign rule except the Holy One. And finally, a domain of faith within whose limits only the individual is Sovereign, and through that faith consecrates himself with his whole being.[34]

Kuyper was here referring to fundamental dimensions of the human experience and "wanted to make clear that 'our human life . . . is neither simple nor uniform, but constitutes an infinitely complex organism.'"[35] Indeed, Kuyper's main concern in relation to articulating idea the notion of distinct spheres was not to map out a curriculum of multidisciplinary study, but to argue for a pluralist society (a "community of communities," in the phrase of his contemporary, the Anglo-Catholic philosopher John Neville Figgis) over and against a unitary, hierarchical, totalizing state.[36]

But did not Kuyper teach that it is important for there to be *Christians* in all areas of life? That if there is a "sphere of commerce," then should there not be *Christian* merchants? And, if this is true, then should there not be a place where people can *train* to be Christian merchants? This is probably the most ambiguous part of Kuyper's thought. Craig Bartholomew, who is warmly appreciative of Kuyper on numerous points, admits that he "never developed a logically tight theory of sphere sovereignty, even though it was

---

33. Harnick, "A Historian's Comment," 282. See also Wells and Bratt, "Piety and Progress," in Hughes and Adrian, eds., *Models*, 138.
34. Kuyper, "Sphere Sovereignty."
35. Harnick, "A Historian's Comment," 282.
36. Tuininga, "Abraham Kuyper," 345–7.

central to his social philosophy."[37] Clearly if we take Kuyper's affirmation of God-normed spheres to mean that the spheres exist under the Lordship of Christ (even if the individuals within them do not acknowledge Christ) then there is not really a need for *Christian* business people, or *Christian* engineers. Those spheres of business and science are *already* under Christ's Lordship—it is Christ, not Christians, who calls them "mine!" On the other hand, these spheres are populated by individuals who do not know Christ. Kuyper argues that Christians possess a clearer vision of the true nature and goal of each of the spheres. Therefore, argues James Bratt, Kuyper thought that Christians must "take [their] claims into the public arena, there to negotiate, repel or sustain as need be."[38] Craig Bartholomew agrees, arguing that for Kuyper "the Christian responsibility is to engage in these spheres in such a way that they become healthier and directed rightly so that they flourish in the best sense of the word."[39] Yet Bartholomew immediately clarifies what this meant: "Kuyper . . . and his colleagues fought for the possibility of alternative Christian organizations in all spheres of life: education, politics, broadcasting, youth organizations, and so on."[40] On this reading, Christians should not go into the existing social structures with the hope of redeeming them as much as establish alternative Christian organizations to reflect God's intent for each sphere of existence. "Kuyper not only wanted us to recognize the different spheres in society but to be intensely aware that different world-views will shape life in these spheres differently."[41] James Bratt concurs. While Kuyper believed that "some of the same stones or joists" could be shared between believers and nonbelievers he nonetheless argued that Christians would "put them in different places and to different purposes in their finished structures, thus in a real sense altering the components themselves."[42]

Kuyper was, in fact, very radical on this point, arguing that regeneration (or *pallingenesis*) "breaks humanity in two, and repeals the unity of the human consciousness . . . And the fact that there are two kinds of *people* occasions of necessity the fact of two kinds of human *life* and *consciousness* of life, and of two kinds of *science*; for which reason the idea of the *unity of*

37. Bartholomew, *Contours*, 106.
38. Wells and Bratt, "Piety and Progress," in Hughes and Adrian, eds., *Models*, 138.
39. Bartholomew, *Contours*, 144.
40. Kuyper, *Encyclopedia*, 224
41. Bartholomew, *Contours*, 144.
42. Bratt, *Abraham Kuyper*, 211–12.

science, taken in its absolute sense, implies the denial of the facts of palingenesis, and therefore from principle leads to the rejection of the Christian religion."[43] Thus, in response to calls to establish Christian chairs at secular universities, Kuyper warned against "sauntering around another garden, clipper in hand," an observation, which if extended to other spheres of life, would suggest he did not want to insert Christians into otherwise secular professions in the hope of pruning and lopping them into shape. To do this, he said "is to throw away the dignity of the Christian religion."[44]

I think much of what Evangelical colleges propose their students will do when they graduate might fall under Kuyper's description of "sauntering around another garden, clipper in hand." Evangelical colleges tend to take Kuyper to mean that one can do business, or engineering, or cyber-security as long as you do it for Jesus. By this they mean that the individual will act "Christianly" within the basically secular profession into which they are entering. In such a construal the focus will naturally fall more on the personal character of the individual than any kind of Kuyperian wholesale reappraisal of the underlying assumptions upon which the profession is based, let alone of the society in which the profession operates.

This means that despite invoking Kuyper's name, I do not think that Kuyperianism really is the dominant philosophy at most Evangelical colleges. Rather Evangelical colleges use Kuyper's notion of God's holistic sovereignty to justify their multidisciplinary catalog. This aphoristic use of Kuyper has been particularly useful to those Evangelical colleges that have evolved from a Bible school or Fundamentalist heritage because it explains why a Christian college now teaches "secular" subjects. However, few of these colleges undertake the kind of reconstructionism of epistemological foundations, or promote the building of alternative Christian social organizations, that is seemingly required by Kuyperian theology. There are two reasons for this failure.

First, Evangelical Christianity has often taken a pragmatic approach to work and vocation. It sees a need for Christians in multiple arenas of life and work primarily so that individuals can be salt and light—influencers or evangelists. However, unlike Kuyperianism properly defined, the Evangelical tradition doesn't see any of these arenas as *intrinsically* important within the divine economy. If one's personal integrity can be maintained in these professions (don't become a drug dealer or prostitute, don't lie and cheat),

---

43. Kuyper, *Encyclopedia*, 154; Bratt, *Abraham Kuyper*, 210–11
44. Bartholomew, *Contours*, 146.

then they are permissible occupations, though not particularly intrinsically significant. The Evangelical does not particularly want to reconstruct the world as much as go into it to help as many individuals as possible be reconciled to God. Ironically, precisely because Evangelicalism has always privileged saving souls for the *world to come,* it is happy to take the current world as it is—as long as the individual Christian avoids flagrant sin that might compromise their salvation.[45] The Evangelical college is therefore congenitally uninterested in reconstructing the foundational assumptions of disciplines, professions, or spheres, and is much more eager to reconstruct the *individual* who will work within these spheres. When Evangelical colleges think about why students should study a wide range of subjects, they simply think that there should be individual Christians in all arenas of life to witness to Jesus.

The second, and perhaps more important, reason for eschewing full-orbed Kuyperianism is that Kuyper is too radical. Properly taught and applied Kuyperianism might render students *unable* to participate in the modern economy. Kuyper was not particularly market sensitive. Happily, the Evangelical insouciance to cultural or societal reconstruction rooted in a particular theological understanding of the individual also turns out to be very pragmatic, since it does not seek to challenge or overturn the basic principles of the American capitalist market economy. Evangelical colleges can therefore promise students that they will succeed in their chosen profession as well as learning to see it from a Christian perspective. The result is that one gets a set of majors mirroring the sectorial division of professions in the modern economy justified on high-minded Kuyperian grounds, but which are never really put through the Kuyperian wringer and so emerge looking pretty much the same as they went in, albeit with students who have perhaps been given stronger moral and spiritual foundations as individuals—not a bad thing, but not a Kuyperian thing either.

An example of the slippage between a notional Kuyperian rationale for education and a more traditional Evangelical missionary pragmatism, which is then in turn merged with the promise of marketable skills, can be found in a flyer produced a few years ago by the Gordon College Department of Engineering. The publicity brochure began by quoting Kuyper's "square inch" slogan and involved Kuyper's "grand view of redemption" which, the flyer promised, will be used to help students at Gordon develop a "Christian worldview" about engineering. So far, so Kuyperian. But as

---

45. Bebbington, *Evangelicalism in Modern Britain,* 133–35.

the recruitment spiel goes on, attention turns to the *practical* benefit of the program, promising that a Christian liberal arts college is "the optimal framework from which to prepare the 21st century engineer." This is market-sensitive, not Kuyperian, language. Having thus shifted away from presuppositional questions toward making a promise to deliver strong professional skills and success in the mainstream secular economy, the author of the publicity pamphlet perhaps realized they had lost the Kuyperian thread and so ended on a very different note. The major, concluded the flyer, is actually "preparing missionaries for the engineering mission field."[46] This latter assertion owes less to Abraham Kuyper and more to Gordon's heritage as a missionary training institution founded by the nineteenth-century missionary Adoniram Judson Gordon. What started as Kuyperian theology promising a Christian worldview ends with a vision of engineering as an Evangelical mission field. And, by a happy coincidence, this mission field is also one of the best paid professional sectors in the United States!

The basic value proposition of the Evangelical college is not Kuyperianism but individualistic Jesusy neoliberalism.[47] Evangelical colleges promise to cultivate that "inner type of identity that will allow [the student] not lose a sense of who he is even while he is being successful in Nebuchadnezzar's court."[48] This analogy (stated positively by its authors) is very revealing. It does indeed capture what Evangelical college often promises its students, but it of course misunderstands the biblical story to which it alludes. Daniel was a "success" at the court of the idolatrous Babylonian king only after he *denounced* the hubris and idol worship of the monarch. He was not therefore "successful" in the way that an Evangelical college promises that students can blend inner piety with outward success in the court of the American economy. Daniel did not develop a Christ-centered worldview while also gaining the skills that would get him an entry-level job in the Golden Calf Corporation.

Financial exigencies (and a certain tension present even within the "purest" form of Kuyperianism) means that even neo-Calvinist colleges with a more overt and systematic commitment to Kuyperianism might also end up in a place where they appear to validate, rather than reconstruct, the prevailing assumptions of the society in which they operate. While some

46. Gordon College, "Gordon College Engineering."

47. This phrase echoes Mark Galli's ascription of Evangelicalism as a "Jesus-y" movement. Galli, "Anvil of the Evangelical Mind."

48. Glanzer et al., *Restoring*, 311.

so-called "antithetical" Kuyperians lean toward those parts of Kuyper's thought that emphasize Christian distinction from, and tension with, the non-Christian world, other "positive" Kuyperians (who have generally won the day within Evangelical higher education) stressed accommodation, co-operation, and co-belligerence with non-Christian society on matters in which "common grace" had created common ground. Don Carson noted the tension existed even within Kuyper's own life. In later life Kuyper drew back from the radical presuppositionalism of his earlier years and entered the political sphere, with all its attendant compromises and negotiations. Yet in being more open to cultural cooperation, the "positive" Kuyperians have faced a challenge of being co-opted by society. Speaking of trends he saw at work at Dordt College, James Burtchaell noted that while some might worry that Kuyperianism turns Christians into arrogant bullies—a critique which might tell against so-called "antithetical" Kuyperians who, following Kuyper, claim only those who have been renewed by the Spirit have truth about how the spheres of society should work—there is also

> a wholly different, sinister, long-term prospect: that the church, if authorized to describe the rationale and the moral guidelines for the mercantile, fiscal, political, educational, artistic, and social projects of such a sober and thrifty people, would be inexorably beguiled to shape its wisdom to its secular constituencies. That would have been a worry of a different sort: that a magisterial Reformed church might become, not a bully, but a shill.[49]

Even James Bratt, sympathetic to the "positive" Kuyperianism that has prevailed at Calvin College/University since the 1970s, admits that Kuyperianism has often appealed to those who wished to "grasp the brass ring of status mobility" while "devot[ing] all their ambitions to the Lord."[50] Writing with Ronald Wells, Bratt lamented that the Christian college has too often catered to those "who hungered for the practical, who would indulge a prettified version of mass culture, who wished to join good pay with inner piety and call it a Christian life."[51] Too often, it seems there is not a square inch of the modern American economy over which the Evangelical college will not promise its students success.

---

49. Burtchaell, *Dying of the Light*, 785.
50. Wells and Bratt, "Piety and Progress," in Hughes and Adrian, eds., *Models*, 139–40.
51. Wells and Bratt, "Piety and Progress," in Hughes and Adrian, eds., *Models*, 149.

Christ and Culture

Let us consider the second thinker who might be invoked to justify a many-splendored catalog, the American theologian H. Richard Niebuhr. Niebuhr's most well-known construct is a taxonomy of five ways in which the church has imagined the relationship between Christ and culture: Christ against culture, Christ of culture, Christ above culture, Christ and culture in paradox, and Christ the transformer of culture. Niebuhr's preference is clearly for the fifth of these models, "Christ the transformer of culture." In fact, since he wrote the definitions, it is not really a fair contest since he clearly wants the final iteration to win and therefore loads the other modes with undesirable characteristics! This phrase is often cited in the literature and self-understanding of Evangelical higher education, although Niebuhr enjoys less name recognition than Kuyper.[52]

The concept of cultural transformation has been useful to Evangelical colleges for reasons like those that help explain why Kuyper's square inch aphorism is readily cited. On the one hand, the notion keeps intact the traditional Evangelical language of activism and conversionism, albeit now rebranded under the moniker of "cultural transformation." On the other hand, the idea of transforming culture sounds broader and more sophisticated than the older Bible college idea of training missionaries to save souls. Furthermore, since transforming culture involves students becoming engaged with multiple arenas of society this idea justifies the fact that Evangelical colleges are engaged in teaching many different disciplinary and professional programs.[53] The idea of Christians transforming culture might also appeal to an element of Evangelicalism that has pictured Christians as involved in battle for control of key political and social institutions. This "culture war" movement, dominant since the 1970s, can itself be construed as a modern variation on a desire to forge a Christian society that stretches back to the "benevolent empire" of Bible societies, mission agencies, and moral reform movements of the nineteenth century, which in turn had its roots in the energies unleashed by the Great Awakening of the mid-eighteenth century. This element of Evangelicalism might be seen to be in certain contradiction to individualistic character of Evangelicalism described in the previous section. However, when Evangelicals have engaged cultural

---

52. For a survey of Evangelical colleges, institutions and writers who invoke Niebuhr's "Christ transforming culture" slogan, see Wittmer, "Analysis and Critique," 1.

53. Bratt and Wells, "Piety and Progress," in Hughes and Adrian, eds., *Models*, 152.

issues in this way it has typically been focused on a somewhat narrow array of issues perceived to have obvious moral or religious significance, rather than flowing from any kind of holistic vision for the divine significance of all creation. Cultural transformation is therefore often selective, and is often aimed at getting public institutions, government, or the legal system to endorse or support certain Evangelical precepts. Evangelical cultural transformation tends to be less a vision of fundamental cultural reimagination and more a series of campaigns and crusades about specific issues that are exorcising the Evangelical community.

Registering the longevity of this Evangelical vision of cultural transformation means that, despite sometimes quoting Niebuhr, Evangelical colleges have probably not actually *learned* the basic attitude about transforming culture *from* Niebuhr. A concept of "cultural transformation" has always been part of the American Evangelical heritage. In fact, as Michael Wittmer has argued, Niebuhr's understanding of "Christ transforming culture" is markedly different to the typical Evangelical construal of this concept. While the Evangelical vision of cultural transformation is the redemption of *certain things within* a zone called "culture," Niebuhr was more concerned with the ontological transformation of human culture by God-in-Christ. For Niebuhr, Christ stood in solidarity with all people and therefore transformed the very essence of culture and thus the very essence *of humanity*. This was a stance Niebuhr learned from the nineteenth-century theologian Anglican F. D. Maurice, with whom he shared belief that Christ would bring all people to salvation (i.e., universalism).

Niebuhr's understanding of the transformation of culture in Christ was not in any straightforward way a template for how *Christians* should transform culture. Rather it was a statement about the eternal reconciliation between humanity and God that Niebuhr believed had been achieved in Christ. As for what Christian actions flowed from this new reality Niebuhr was in fact somewhat vague. He even seemed to argue Christians could not actually do much to change the world—he styled this "The Grace of Doing Nothing"—although he did argue that the church could perhaps help the world clear away its idols in to open space for all people to realize the new divine reality. Since he listed capitalism as among the false gods that the church was meant to topple, I am skeptical that he would have endorsed the Evangelical college setting up market-oriented professional programs and invoking his "Christ the transformer of culture" slogan to justify them.[54]

---

54. Wittmer, "Analysis and Critique," 129, 264.

I think, then, we can quite easily dispense with Niebuhr himself as a witness against my argument. Not only does his vision of Christ and culture not comport with what most Evangelical colleges understand by the term, but elements of his theological vision stand in opposition to the prevailing protocols of Christian higher education. But what of the broader Evangelical belief that Christians must transform culture, the attitude that Niebuhr's slogan is assumed (not quite accurately, as it turns out) to exemplify? Is *this* an idea that legitimates a broad-spectrum catalog? The question here is twofold. First, is cultural transformation a worthy goal? Second, are Evangelical colleges set up to achieve it?

In answer to the first question, the "irony and tragedy" of the kind of cultural transformation to which White American Evangelicals have often aspired has been described powerfully by James Davison Hunter. Hunter contends that aspiring to change the culture always requires Christians grasping for power, a reflex that inevitably corrupts and distorts the gospel. This is especially the case when, as has been common among American Evangelicals, cultural transformation is construed as involving changing laws and government. The cultural transformation agenda tends to secularize Christianity more than it sacralizes the culture. This is because the culture defines the methods and delineates the possible outcomes. As Christians work within these parameters, they bend their identity and vision into conformity with mechanisms needed to effect social and cultural change. Inasmuch as Evangelical colleges are adjunct to the broader culture wars that rage in the United States, they therefore run the danger of secularization by the culture, even as they aspire to transform it.

Regarding the second question: are Christian colleges structured to achieve cultural transformation? Even if one believed in the concept of cultural transformation to be a valid objective it is dubious how much cultural transformation an Evangelical college could expect its students to achieve when it has itself spent four years acculturating students to the professional norms of the modern American economy. I once observed a class in sports marketing that was part of a sports management degree. The professor told the students that sports marketing was often duplicitous and based on false ideas of body image and that Christians ought to resist. But exactly what was the student meant to do with this information? Why is the college offering a sports marketing class if the prevailing protocols of this profession are unethical? It might be replied that it is hoped that Christ-centered students will change this practice and redeem the profession. However, it is unrealistic to expect a junior employee will be able to resist such unethical practices. It is much more likely that, during their formative years in the profession, lacking agency and authority, the student would become desensitized and acculturated to the problematic practices of the industry. In other words, Evangelical colleges may speak about cultural transformation, but they do not construct their curriculum with much serious attention to changing the culture. Instead, when they speak about cultural transformation, they tend to really mean *individual* transformation—or, at most, the aggregate result of transformed individuals—operating within the regular spheres of modern life.

But perhaps this idea of helping the individual grow in their personal virtue and ethical fortitude is close to Hunter's concept of *faithful presence*, the paradigm that he proposes as an alternative to the "cultural transformation" concept? Is the Evangelical college legitimized in having a multi-orbed curriculum so that it can encourage students to be a "faithful presence" within multiple spheres of life?

It is difficult to draw such a conclusion. "Faithful presence," as construed by Hunter, is not limited to the faithful presence of one individual in one sector or profession but to the presence of Christians as a community within "the context of complex social, political, economic and cultural forces."[55] "Faithful presence" does not simply take this bundle of forces and aspire to to inhabit them "faithfully." Rather faithful presence requires a high degree of discernment about how to live in what are a bundle of contradictory cultural webs. Simply replicating threads of these webs within an Evangelical college catalog and then talking about being faithful within them is insufficient.[56]

---

55. Hunter, *To Change the World*, 198.

56. Brad East is somewhat more critical of Hunter, arguing that his "presentation of 'faithful presence within' suffers from an overly sanguine view of the professions and institutions in which Christians are called to be present." East sees Hunter as merely rebranding the Kuyperian (or perhaps we can say ersatz-Kuyperian) idea that everything can be done for God—the idea that I have argued is used to justify a range of market-sensitive programs at most Evangelical colleges. Thus, argues East, Hunter "does not prepare believers to consider all the ways their faith will require them not to participate in the workforce, not to attain lucrative careers, not to benefit from the economy, not to 'engage' the culture. At the end of the day, even when it nods at critique, it is a social ethic of relentless affirmation and only modest, and then partial and incrementalist, antithesis." While I think Hunter is somewhat more prophetic than East allows, I of course concur with East that the issue of *what Christians cannot do* is one that needs much more attention when thinking about what makes a Christian college Christian. East, "Once More."

In fact, in affirmation of my basic thesis, the notion of "faithful presence," as Hunter conceives of it, is the work not simply of individuals but of the *church*. The church, argues Hunter, must commit to a "thorough critique of the modern world," a process that he argues has not yet begun and which "it would take many talented scholars many years to achieve."[57] Next, the church must adopt a posture of critical and prophetical engagement with the culture. "The church, as it exists within the wide range of individual vocations in very sphere of social life (commerce, philanthropy, education, etc.) must be present in the world in ways that work toward the *constructive* subversion of all frameworks of social life that are incompatible with the shalom for which we were made to which we are called." In practice, argues Hunter, given what we know of the cultural malaise in which we live "this means that the church and its people must stand in a position of critical reistance to late modernity and its dominant institutions and carriers; institutions like modern capitalism, liberalism, social theory, health care, urban planning, architecture, art, moral formation, and family and so on . . . in order to offer an alternative vision and direction from them."[58] Finally, (and I think most saliently) Hunter points out that all cultural critique should not actually begin *out there* but *in here*. It is the *church* that needs liberating from cultural captivity, not the culture. "Nowhere is this task of critical resistance more urgent than the Christian church itself for the ways that it too has accomodated to the late modern age," argues Hunter.[59] In other words, the mission of the church to be a prophetic, subversive force in the culture can only be achieved if the church itself has a cultural transformation.

The Evangelical college could and should help the church with this urgent renewal of self-critique and, thence, aid the church in its mission of constructive subversion. But the Evangelical itself has accomodated itself to late modernity and therefore lacks the intellectual, spiritual, and moral capacity to engage in critically resisting the very frameworks of social life that it has inscribed in its own academic catalogs. Moreover, as I will argue in chapters 3 and 4, since the Christian college sees "Christianity" (cast in the Evangelical mold) as the basic value-added dimension to its educational offerings, it finds it almost impossible to *critique* the defeciencies of the Christian tradition of which it is a part, and which it markets as its most notable distinctive in the crowded higher educational marketplace.

57. Hunter, *To Change the World*, 199.
58. Hunter, *To Change the World*, 235–36.
59. Hunter, *To Change the World*, 236.

Christ and the Catalog

All Truth Is God's Truth

There is one final phrase that might tell against my protestations concerning the secularity of the catalog: "All truth is God's truth." This phrase is often used to make the same kind of totalizing claim as that implied by Kuyper's "square inch" dictum, although when scrutinized in detail it carries different theological freight. Indeed, the phrase "all truth is God's truth" is in one sense diametrically opposed to Kuyperian principles. Kuyper explicitly denied that real truth could be found outside of an approach to truth that began with a fully orbed set of philosophical and epistemological presuppositions derived from the Christian worldview (although, as noted above, there is an in-house debate on this matter between self-avowed Kuyperians). This phrase "all truth is God's truth" makes the opposite point. The truth is out there and can be found even among those who have not based their search for truth on reconstructed Christian presuppositions.

This third view has enjoyed great salience in church history. It was utilized as an apologetic tool by the early church to suggest that the philosophies of pre-Christian Greco-Roman culture contained elements of truth and that the pagan philosophers were "Christians before Christ." John Calvin later captured this long-standing belief: "As truth is most precious, so all men confess it to be so. And yet, since God alone is the source of all good, you must not doubt, that whatever truth you anywhere meet with, proceeds from Him, unless you would be doubly ungrateful to Him."[60]

The statement that "all truth is God's truth" is, of course, irrefragably true because, if one has a basic understanding of God as the author of truth, then the phrase is a truism—and all truisms are God's truisms! But while it is true that all truth is God's truth, this does not mean everything is true; nor, to put it ethically, does it mean that everything is right. This slogan cannot therefore justify *doing anything and everything*. As Frank E. Gaebelein, one of the earliest champions of this maxim in modern Evangelical education, realized: "All truth is GOD'S TRUTH, but how to determine the truth—as Hamlet said, 'there's the rub.'"[61] The assertion that all truth is God's truth, while legitimating a curriculum that spans beyond biblical studies and theology, does not help in determining what or what not the Christian college should be validating as *true*. Indeed, if one adheres to

---

60. Bill J. Leonard, "What Can the Baptist Tradition Contribute to Christian Higher Education? Christian Identity and Academic Rigor: The Case of Samford University," in Hughes and Adrian, eds., *Models*, 378.

61. Beck, "All Truth," 104.

this principle, then one would expect all disciplines to produce a mixture of truth and error. If one believes that all truth is God's truth, then one must also believe that it is the job of teaching and learning *to discern that truth*—to sort the gold from the dross. In the Christian humanist tradition, the point of studying non-Christian texts was not so that one could then become assimilated to the overall identity or posture of the person who produced that gem of truth but rather so that one could claim that truth for the Christian church. It was for this reason that the early church fathers talked of "plundering the Egyptians," not of walking like them. The Christian humanist tradition therefore maintains a position of skepticism about what it is encountering.[62]

However, this approach becomes very difficult to sustain if one is pursuing a degree program that offers one training to *do* something. It is not clear that the notion of all truth being God's truth can be translated to training for professional accreditation since it is premised on education being an act of critical engagement and reflection on the ideas and actions of others, an education that knows when to embrace and when to refrain from embracing. By contrast, professional training involves submitting oneself to be *molded into conformity* with a set of externally derived values and aptitudes. In the context of professional training, one does not have the luxury of picking and choosing what is common-grace truth, and what is the result of sinful distortion. Rather, one must swallow the package whole. As Robert Brimlow argues,

> The fundamental and inescapable point of professional education is to enable practitioners to work better . . . The purpose and goal of professional programs is to ensure that students who complete the course of study are admitted into practice; this is the defining measure of a program's success . . . The programs are designed to facilitate the understanding, acceptance, and conformity to the social roles of practitioners as defined by the socially derived standards.[63]

Lest my argument sounds like a jeremiad against professional training in favor of liberal arts, it is worth noting that one could make a similar critique against a purely classical curriculum, especially given the tendency

---

62. Brimlow, "Who Invited Mammon?," in Budde and Wright, eds., *Conflicting Allegiances*, 162.

63. Brimlow, "Who Invited Mammon?," in Budde and Wright, eds., *Conflicting Allegiances* 166–67.

of some Christians to uncritically baptize the classics as a foundation of "Christian civilization," or to invest literary or philosophical notions with Christian rhetoric. Will Herberg (1901–1977) once asked why his Christian friends clung to "a thinly Christianized version of the Greek ideal of intellectual seal-realization . . . If man's good was the 'life according to reason,' as it was in the classics-humanistic ideal, then a liberal education along academic lines was obviously appropriate; but how appropriate was it, indeed what sense did it make, if man's good was what the Christian faith must hold it to be—to know and do the will of God?"[64] Augustine warned that "we were seduced and we seduced others . . . both openly by the so-called liberal arts and secretly in the name of a false religion, proud in the one, superstitious in the other, and everywhere vain."[65]

My point here is not that liberal arts *defined as a corpus or body of work* is free from the risk of secularization; rather, it is that the classic suite of liberal arts disciplines (literature, history, philosophy) model a mode of inquiry—skeptical and discerning, discriminating, and critical—that avoid the student being consumed by and conformed to the *content* of these studies in a way that is not available to professional training. Other more modern academic disciplines—sociology, anthropology, cultural and media studies—can also model this methodological discernment. It is not therefore my argument that we must defend the classic humanities-based liberal arts and exclude all other disciplines, but rather that, as V. James Mannoia argues, Christian colleges must ensure we privilege the *liberating arts*.[66] We must make a distinction between education that liberates and education that acculturates.[67] For Christians, the liberating potential of education is that it can free us of our accreted, habitual, stultified identities and behaviors in order that we can embrace with less encumbrance or hindrance our identity and calling as the members of the people of God.

A vision of an education that liberates was the essence of the model set out by Arthur Holmes in his seminal book *The Idea of a Christian College*. Unlike Kuyperians, the Anglican Arthur Holmes was concerned not so much with teaching *from* a Christian worldview but using the disciplinary ecumenism of a liberal arts curriculum to help students build *toward* a

64. Burtchaell, *Dying of the Light*, 821.
65. Glanzer et al., *Restoring the Soul*, 263.
66. Mannoia, "Christian Higher Education."
67. On the notion of the "liberating arts" in general, see Bilbro et al., eds., *Liberating Arts*.

Christian worldview.[68] Worldview is a work in progress—"exploratory . . . an endless undertaking that is still but the vision of a possibility, an unfinished symphony barely begun."[69] To achieve this end Holmes realized that it would not be enough to offer an eclectic range of majors from a Christian perspective and ask individual professors to ensure they were taught from a Christian worldview. He saw the need for an integrative center. Holmes's basic conviction of *how* this integration happened was rooted in a classic understanding of liberal arts education tuned to Christian ends. Education was a way of harvesting and harmonizing multiple disciplinary insights into a coherent, vivifying vision of the world.[70]

Whither this vision of the Evangelical college? The liberal arts and humanities are under massive pressure across the entire higher education sector. Evangelical colleges do not seem interested in defending them, instead letting them wither in favor of more market-sensitive programs.[71] Already by 1990 there were more students in professional programs than in traditional liberal arts disciplines at Calvin College. Richard Mouw, who had championed the expansion of professional programs in the 1970s, departed Calvin worrying that "many new programs threatened precisely [the] liberal arts center and with it the vitality of the collegiate enterprise."[72] It is true that the humanities departments may still contribute to "general education" or "core" requirements, but they are often pictured as providing *foundations* rather than *summations* of learning. Students coming to the end of their majors rarely return to their general education classes to have the content of their forty-five or so credits of work in the major put into conversation with the integrative humane disciplines. Indeed, humanities disciplines are often treated as just one major among many. They are asked to prove how *they* integrate faith and learning as a single discipline but are not viewed by the institution as the context in which *all* integrative activity must take place. As John Fea observes "our heady conversations about the 'evangelical mind' seem futile in the face of steep declines in the number of

68. VanZanten, *Joining the Mission*, 112.
69. Holmes, *Idea of a Christian College*, 58.
70. I will return to the concept of "worldview" in the next chapter.
71. This diminution of liberal arts is not unique to Evangelical colleges. A study in 2012 found about one-third of colleges that had called themselves liberal arts in 1990 no longer meet that description due to the addition of professional programs. I know of no comparable study of Christian colleges, but I suspect the proportions would be similar. Baker et al., "Where Are They Now?"
72. Bratt and Wells, "Piety and Progress," in Hughes and Adrian, eds., *Models*, 156.

students studying these [liberal arts disciplines] beyond the general education curriculum."[73]

This relegation and diminution of humanities and liberal arts as the hub of integration has a parallel in the surprising lack of Bible, religion, and theology classes on Evangelical college campuses. A commitment to adjudicating between truth and error in multiple disciplines, as the "all truth is God's truth" aphorism invites one to do, should lead to the Bible and religion department playing a central, integrative role. However, Bible departments are shrinking, and Evangelical colleges appear willing to cull faculty and programs in these areas. In his study of Dordt College, James Burtchaell found that the Dutch department offered as many classes as the Bible department, agriculture offered twice as many, business three times more, and the education department four times as many. "Granted the repeated claim that the Bible is the fundamental source of Christian faith and critical insight, it is astonishing to find . . . little exposure to a contextual reading of the books themselves."[74] While Evangelical colleges may offer Bible classes as foundational requirements, the Bible and religion department is rarely mandated to come alongside *all* disciplines to offer theological and biblical perspective. Indeed, in what is an odd professional division of labor, the person whom the Evangelical college makes responsible for helping students find ways that the Bible connects with a nonbiblical academic discipline is rarely the person who possess a PhD in biblical studies, but the professor who may never have studied the Bible beyond more than personal or church Bible study level. As I will argue in the next chapter, in such a scenario what inevitably ends up being claimed as the "Christian perspective" can be a simplistic and sub-biblical version of Christianity that does injustice to the riches of Scripture and Christian doctrine.

CONCLUSION

While each of the three approaches surveyed above has its own strengths and weaknesses, the basic premise of each paradigm captures an essential point about the relationship of God to the created order and impels Christians toward integrated thinking and holistic living. However, none of the three philosophies can straightforwardly justify or legitimate the really existing Evangelical college. In fact, each has significant elements that tell

---

73. Fea, "What is the State of the Evangelical Mind?"
74. Burtchaell, *Dying of the Light*, 806.

against the prevailing practices of many Christian higher education institutions. Each approach demands a far more systematic, holistic, and even subversive approach to both the form, content, and *telos* of the educational endeavor than is common at most Evangelical colleges. None of the approaches promise economic success or marketable skills. Rather, all invite a deeply critical and prophetic posture toward regnant social, economic, and cultural forms. While the invocation of these visions of education might at first seem to be a rejoinder to the accusations that I have leveled against the Evangelical college, I believe that if the proponents of these visions were called to the stand they would turn witness for the prosecution.

Given that Kuyper and friends do not justify the practices of the Evangelical college, I therefore remain committed to my claim that the overarching programmatic offerings of the Evangelical college are cut from the same cloth as most nonreligious universities. Programs are added or subtracted on market grounds, and colleges promise students employability and success. Appeals to the holistic nature of Christian truth as the rationale for a many-splendored catalog mask the fact that students are in fact channeled into relatively narrow disciplinary, professional, and technical fields. While *taken as a whole* the college catalog might be argued to exemplify the fact that every square inch belongs to God, or that all truth is God's truth, an *individual student* will only take up residence in a narrow plot within this broad dominion. Neither the content nor form of the curriculum are shaped according to any theological or missiological precepts, and even some administrators appear to recognize that the Evangelical college is in thrall to market in ways that compromise its mission.

The reader might concede some or much of this argument. However, many will insist that the real distinction of the Evangelical college is that every subject *within* the catalog is taught from a Christian perspective. It is this vision of bringing faith into learning that has animated much of what has been written about Evangelical higher education and which shapes the imagination of both faculty and administrators about what makes the Evangelical college distinctive. It is therefore to this concept that I now turn.

Chapter 3

The Disintegration of Faith and Learning

A DOMINANT CONCEPT IN Christian higher education has been the idea of the "integration" of the Christian faith with the content of academic classes. Although the phrase "integration of faith and learning" is a cliché that has been subject to critique among scholars who write on Christian pedagogy, the concept still enjoys widespread affirmation among many faculty and administrators. It has been described as the "calling card" of the CCCU.[1] In their 2014 study of CCCU faculty, Samuel Joeckel and Thomas Chesnes found that 80 percent of faculty believed they practiced the integration faith and learning.[2]

Exactly how this interplay between faith and learning should be realized is a hazier matter. There is a bewildering array of models of faith-learning integration. Preston B. Cosgrove identified thirty-seven varieties of faith-learning integration, many laboring under neologisms such as "Correlational," "Compatibilist," "Convergence" and "Foundational" approaches. Whether any of these models can be found in pure form in the classroom is dubious. As Lyon et al. observe, "the integration of faith and learning is typically more popular in theory than in practice."[3] In her study of faith integration at a Christian college, Constance Chibuzo Nwosu concluded that professors often "defined [the integration of faith and learning]

---

1. Allen and Badley, *Faith and Learning*, 23.
2. Allen and Badley, *Faith and Learning*, 13–17.
3. Lyon et al., "Making sense," 337.

based on their everyday life as Christians and professionals rather than what the books said."[4] Most faculty probably do not adopt a particular "model" of Christian education.[5] A lot of faith-learning integration is intuitive and improvised. It may also be muddy and confused. "Many faculty passionately believe in the call to integrate faith and learning," observes Lori Kanitz, "yet they find it difficult to know whether they are actually doing it, and, more importantly, whether they have succeeded."[6] Indeed, dig a little deeper into the literature and it is surprising how many people acknowledge that faith-learning integration is a problem in Evangelical colleges. Michael S. Hamilton has observed that "despite thirty years of talk about integration of faith and learning, and despite a half-dozen best-selling books that call on Christians to take intellectual life more seriously, the idea of Christian scholarship remains elusive for women and men who teach at and who lead Christian colleges and universities."[7] Given the centrality of the concept to the identity and "brand" of the Evangelical college this confession is a bit like Coca-Cola employees admitting they don't actually quite know how to make the stuff.[8]

Even if faculty feel that they *are* confident at performing faith-learning integration, it is unclear whether the results are always laudable. As James Patterson has observed, "The pursuit of such integration is commendable; unhappily, the reality on many Christian campuses does not match the ideal."[9] Some visions of integration are, to put it bluntly, shallow, banal, confused, and probably entirely counterproductive. To take one example, after surveying ways in which graphic design professors integrated faith and learning, Lorraine Bower reported that

> one respondent took up the biblical concept of the believer being branches that are pruned by God in an allusion to John 15:1–2: "I am the true vine, and my Father is the gardener. He cuts off every branch in me that bears no fruit, while every branch that does bear fruit he prunes so that it will be even more fruitful" . . . For me I

4. Nwosu, "Integration," 78.

5. Here Ream and Glanzer make somewhat heavy weather of their revised formulation "Christ-infused learning." While the phrase is fresh, I'm not sure it is as distinct from what is generically meant by integration of faith and learning as they presume. Ream and Glanzer, *Idea of a Christian College*, 53–55.

6. Kanitz, "Improving," 99.

7. Hamilton, "Reflection," 13.

8. Tolbert "Exploration."

9. Patterson, "Boundary Maintenance," 54.

> often relate design to what God is doing in our own lives in that we have to edit our work a lot and cut out what is not necessary . . . and I think that is how I get them to see design as well. Like, "Is this necessary? If it's not, just leave it off."[10]

This is pseudo-integration. It takes a biblical passage, strips it of its context, and then turns it into an allegory for editing a movie. A verse that is all about Jesus (Christ-centered, one might say) becomes a metaphor about how to cut and splice a film. In the same study, Bower quoted a professor in design who liked

> to point out [to students] how prayer works in solving creative problems . . . When I was working in the industry and I had to come up with a solution to a design problem, probably you would call it unconscious thinking, but I would feed all the requirements and data to myself . . . then I would pray for a creative answer . . . and then I would forget about it . . . and at three in the morning, it would come to me. Nine times out of ten the first thing I would come up with would be what the client would want.[11]

Here God is presented as a divine afflatus, granting ideas to help a designer aid their clients. But what do the clients want to design? Is it something that benefits the kingdom of God? Will God always grant you such inspiration? There is minimal reflection on any such broader questions, nor any actual link to biblical theology. Oddly, while Lorraine Bower seems to recognize the problems with these approaches, her conclusion is not that graphic design professors need to read more theology but rather that theologians need spend more time thinking about graphic design![12] There are no doubt better examples of integration than this, but given that these were published in a leading peer-reviewed journal, I expect there are also worse.

One of the problems at play here is that most faculty lack training in biblical exegesis, hermeneutics, or theological practice. The sole criteria for teaching at an Evangelical college is that one enjoys a personal relationship with Jesus. This means that, as Douglas Jacobsen and Rhonda Hustedt Jacobsen observe, "Many Christians are just as unreflective about the ways their faith interacts with their scholarship as anyone else in the academy. . . While they have developed detailed and nuanced understandings of their academic disciplines, many have allowed reflection on faith to languish at a

---

10. Bower, "Faith-Learning," 18.
11. Bower, "Faith-Learning," 18.
12. Bower, "Faith-Learning," 25.

Sunday School level of insight."[13] Their point is echoed by Harold Heie, who observes that "our own theological sophistication as faculty members outside the field of theology often does not exceed the advanced Sunday school level."[14] Given this, it is almost inevitable that what will be rendered as a "Christian" or "biblical" perspective on a given topic is liable to be theologically problematic or biblically unwarranted. As James Burtchaell noted: "It is quite common for evangelical colleges to claim that they integrate faith with learning [but one] quickly notices, however, that Scripture is not all the source for these ventures at integration. Nor are they very theological."[15]

The problem does not merely subsist in the lack of theological acumen of the faculty, however. Even those with high theological literacy might struggle with the assigned task. This is because the parameters of integration are set by the subject rather than flowing organically from the narrative or priorities of biblical theology. Because the curriculum of any given program in the Evangelical college is determined by the contours of that discipline, Christian faculty are always seeking to link the Bible to the topic of the day. Professors are constantly asking: "'Where is Christ in this?' or 'what's the Christian perspective on this?' . . . the same question in every course offered on campus, regardless of its material: How might a Christian understand this?"[16] Such questions sound like they are giving Christ preeminence by always reminding students to develop a Christian view of each and every thing. However, it also means that the discipline, not the Bible, sets the agenda for the conversation. This approach does not guarantee that the central story and challenge of the gospel will ever be heard in its own voice or on its own terms. It could be an exercise in missing the point. This approach to faith and learning has similarities with how missiologist and Old Testament scholar Christopher Wright describes a common approach to the Bible in general:

> We often ask "where does God fit into my life?" when the real question is "where does my little life fit into this great story of God's mission?" . . . We talk about the problems of "applying the Bible to our lives," which often means modifying the Bible somewhat

---

13. Douglas Jacobsen and Rhonda Hustedt Jacobsen, "More than 'Integration' of Faith and Learning," in Jacobsen and Jacobsen, eds., *Scholarship and Christian Faith*, 18–19.

14. Harold Heie, "What Can the Evangelical/Interdenominatonal Tradition Contribute to Christian Higher Education?" in Hughes and Adrian, eds., *Models*, 259.

15. Burtchaell, *Dying of the Light*, 803.

16. Joeckel and Chesnes, eds., *Christian College Phenomenon*, 9.

The Disintegration of Faith and Learning

adjectivally to fit into the assumed "reality" of the life we live "in the real world." What would it mean to apply our lives to the Bible instead, assuming *the Bible* to be the reality—the real story—to which *we* are called to conform ourselves?[17]

An extended illustration of how the Christian faith can be distorted as one attempts to link it to a pre-existing subject—the contours of which are formed entirely from nonbiblical sources—can be found in an article by Melvin Holder, a professor of business at Belhaven University.[18] Holder begins the article by arguing that there needs to be a coherent, curricular plan for integration of faith and learning. He proposes identifying a class within the business major and using it as a framework by which to evangelize and catechize the students. As Holder begins to map his approach, it at first seems that he proposes that each class to be the *occasion* for an evangelistic or biblical discussion. So, the first class is Effective Professional Communication, which Holder argues is the appropriate place to introduce communicating the gospel. It seems that Holder is proposing running a parallel catechism class alongside his business classes. However, from this point forward, rather than the class merely prompting a discussion of the Bible, the Bible is summoned to provide illustrations or case studies of the subject matter of the class. Thus, Holder proposes, Nehemiah should be used "a case study of modern management theory from the fifth century B.C."; a class on Business Law will involve a "comparison of civil and criminal law with Mosaic Law"; the class on Human Resources will scan the Bible for "principles that relate to human resource management issues such as conflict resolution, succession planning, employee training and development, and workplace diversity"; the Advanced Organizational Behavior class will find lessons about "organizational culture, conflict management, attitudes, values, work motivation, job stress, employee performance, and employee development" from the book of Proverbs; and Paul's missionary journeys will be studied "as a model for a business expanding globally by beginning in the local market and ultimately growing into the worldwide marketplace."[19] *We preach Christ crucified: a scandal to the Jews and a model of how to break into emerging Asian markets for the gentiles!*

Such an approach does not allow the gospel to breathe but instead imprisons it within the structure of a sequence of secular classes. When

---

17. Wright, *Mission of God*, 534.
18. Holder, "Comprehensive Biblical Integration,"
19. Holder, "Comprehensive Biblical Integration," 44–46.

the Bible comes into the class, it is viewed entirely anachronistically as a repository of apparently timeless principles for modern management and global business technique. Holder even uses the phrase (derived from Richard Chewning) of "cherry-picking" the Bible for verses as a positive way of integrating faith and learning. It is notable that there is nowhere in this sequence of "comprehensive biblical integration" any mention of the cross and resurrection of Jesus Christ. The Bible comes to students as a book of useful principles for running a business, not as the *evangel* which announces the defeat of sin, death, and the devil by Christ crucified and risen. This illustration suggests that rather than teaching academics from a Christian perspective, Evangelical colleges might end up often teaching Christianity from a disciplinary perspective. The Christ-centered college catechizes students in major-centered Christianity.

Holder, and many faculty like him, are not to blame for this situation. No amount of "models, diagrams, charts, tables, [and] illustrations on how to integrate faith and learning"[20] will help the issue. The problem is that it is hardly actually possible to integrate faith into the warp and woof undergraduate education as currently constructed in most Evangelical colleges. I am not saying that it is *never* possible, but I am saying that the expectation that it should happen as a matter of course is misguided and, in fact, counter-productive. When this expectation is put onto the shoulders of faculty it will inevitably produce strained, shallow, and banal attempts at linking the class topic to Christianity. The result will always trivialize and secularize the gospel.

The basic problem is a mismatch between the grand ideas of faith-learning integration and the quotidian realities of discipline-based undergraduate education. Although the problem tends to get worse in professional and technical fields, my argument here applies to the entire range of academic programs when they are organized by standard disciplinary boundaries. Many of the statements about integration of faith and learning are made at the meta-level, casting a vision for learning in general or a discipline in relation to cosmic divine realities. What's a Christian view of history? What is the significance of music in God's created order? Why should there be Christian social workers? How does biology reflect God's order? By contrast, the average course is such a small part of God's reality that it is not possible to find distinctively Christian things to say about it that have not already been said in a previous class. Is the Christian view of

---

20. Nwosu, "Integration," 50.

audio design different to the Christian view of video production? Is there a different theological rationale for digital marketing different than for print marketing? Is there a different biblical rationale for Early American Literature from Modern American Literature? A patriot might be able to wax lyrical on the admirable qualities of his country, but he would soon tire of having to find celebratory things to say about every subdivision. Day by day, most Christian educators are touring the neighborhoods of their discipline, not delivering orations on overarching principles of reality. An academic major is a very small part of reality, a course within the major is microscopic, and a single one-hour class session is almost sub-atomic. As one participant in the study of faith-learning integration by Constance Chibuzo Nwosu observed:

> Because of the nature of the material he was dealing with the connections one could make were of the same nature and would end up being repetitious. For instance, there are many mechanisms and provisions that are in our bodies for safety. These should point to our Creator as the Designer. He maintained that he had made this point in previous lessons and did not want to overdo it.[21]

It is simply impossible to teach *each class* from a uniquely, distinctively Christian perspective. There is not enough to say. This might be fine, except when one feels under pressure to say something anyway. This pressure might come formally from administrators and evaluation processes, or informally through the implicit expectations of what one is expected to do to count as a successful Christ-centered educator. Fears of "mission drift" might make administrators particularly concerned about monitoring whether the content of classes is thoroughly and demonstrably taught from a Christian perspective, perhaps even assigning quotas of readings or topics that faculty are told to fulfill in terms of integrating Christian or biblical content.

The implicit pressure also flows through the literature on faith and learning, which often makes heady claims about the distinctiveness and superiority of Christ-centered education and casts the professor as the main agent responsible for the success of the project. As Allen and Badley put it, the Evangelical college professor is "on the hook every moment every day" to integrate faith and learning.[22] The compulsion to find some kind of "faith" element in a content that does not naturally or obviously invite

---

21. Nwosu "Integration," 160.
22. Allen and Badley, *Faith and Learning*, 39–40.

can lead to strained, tenuous, or superficial commentary and purported linkages links to the Bible. Some faculty realize this. As one professor explained to Constance Chibuzo Nwosu, she had taken the decision not to "integrate" that day because "the students might have been tired of hearing about everything being spiritualized . . . She did not want to force IFL [Integration of Faith and Learning] in the class and did not want to rob the students of the content of their course."[23]

An interlocutor might at this point contend that there are in fact many books and articles that discuss faith and learning at the disciplinary level. Therefore, my claim that it is difficult to integrate Christian faith within specific subjects is misguided. It is of course true that there is much written about the relationship between Christianity and particular disciplines. However, these works tend to fall into two types, neither of which necessarily help produce a day-in, day-out Christian pedagogy.

First, there are many statements that seek to theologize a discipline or profession. These tend to show how a given discipline is bound to God's created order, how it nurtures skills and dispositions that are consonant with Christian virtues, or how it equips Christians to act in ways appropriate to Christ's kingdom. These statements, which often appear in handbooks about faith and learning, can be rich and illuminating. I agree with many of them. However, by showing how the subject matter revealed by the discipline, or the disciplinary or professional habits inculcated by the study of the subject can be understood to exist within God's created order, or can serve God's redemptive purposes, these approaches tend to encourage Christians *to do the regular business* of that discipline more than they suggest that it is possible to *teach and study that discipline in a particularly "Christian"* way. They might help faculty *position* the disciplines within a Christian view of reality, but they do not necessarily suggest that you can teach the content *from* a Christian perspective. They urge Christians to change their *perception* of a certain academic or professional activity—to place it *within* a Christian understanding of reality—more than they invite Christians to change how they study, learn, teach, or practice the discipline or profession itself. These statements can therefore inform the "first day of class" *apologias* for the discipline that faculty often give students. But they are limited in their ability to transform the day-to-day teaching of the subject. If these texts give specific examples of how the broad precepts could change the actual pedagogy of the class, they typically identify the

---

23. Nwosu, "Integration," 189.

low-hanging fruit, selecting as examples the most obvious topics that bear upon Christian faith, and remaining silent about most of the content.

The second type of writing about the possibility of distinctly Christian disciplinary practices is associated with thinkers who have proposed that Christian scholarship should be rooted in explicitly Christian presuppositions. This approach aims "to examine the deep philosophical presuppositions of the disciplines . . . in order to see whether and to what degree those philosophical presuppositions may overlap, inform, or conflict with the truths of Christian faith expressed in propositional form."[24] It is this approach to which George Marsden referred to when he noted "the triumph—or nearly so—of what may be loosely called Kuyperian presuppositionalism in our community . . . I refer to a style of Christian thought that emphasizes that crucial to the differences that separate Christian worldviews from non-Christian ones are disagreements about pre-theoretical principle, presuppositions, first commitments, or basic beliefs."[25] Marsden's *Outrageous Idea of Christian Scholarship* is the most well-known manifesto for this vision.

There are several things to note about the limitations of this approach for sustaining a distinctly Christian pedagogy. First, the relevance of conversations about Christian scholarship to undergraduate education is debatable. There is a perennial tendency to assume that this literature about faith and scholarship provides a substantial basis for thinking about the nature of Christian undergraduate education. The confusion rests in part on the ambiguity of the word "learning" (as used in phrase "integration of faith and learning"), a word which can sometimes refer to the type of "learning" produced by the "learned" (i.e., academic scholarship) and sometimes to the type of "learning" done by a freshman reviewing the study guide for a class in remedial math. Because the conversation about Christian "learning" has been carried out rather more by scholars than freshman math students, it means that many discussions about Christianity and the disciplines have in fact centered on "the kind of learning that makes faculty learned, rather than learning understood as the pedagogical experiences of students . . . We have placed at the heart of our conversation about calling the question of what it means for us, as Christian academics, to love God

---

24. Jacobsen and Jacobsen, "More Than the 'Integration' of Faith and Learning," in Jacobsen and Jacobsen, eds., *Scholarship and Christian Faith*, 27.

25. Marsden, "State of Evangelical Christian Scholarship," 355.

truly with all our minds."²⁶ However, what is plausible for scholars is not necessarily possible for undergraduates, nor for a faculty member teaching undergraduates. Methodological first-principle reconstructionism is a poor fit for the average college classroom. Kuyper called his students at the Free University of Amsterdam "a holy priesthood of learning." It is hard to imagine assigning this label to the average freshman survey cohort, some of whom haven't even bought the textbook. There has been insufficient attention given to the vast difference between scholarship and pedagogy in discourse about Evangelical higher education.²⁷

Second, even if one accepts that debates about the foundational paradigms of scholarship have some relevance to the classroom, the question of discussing propositional first principles is weighted toward disciplines which already have a strong interest in conversations about the philosophical theory upon which the discipline rests. As Douglas Jacobsen and Rhonda Jacobsen note, while this approach "can be especially helpful when dealing with disciplines that touch on issues that have been of traditional concern to moral faith that is, questions of human origins, meaning and moral values," it "flounders ... when applied either to disciplines that are more naturally descriptive or pragmatic in orientation or to disciplines in which issues of human meaning rarely enter the mix."²⁸ This leads to what Weeks and Isaaks describe as "significant consternation among many faculty members on how to define and implement faith integration in academic disciplines outside of theology, philosophy, Christian ministry, and possibly, nursing."²⁹ V. James Mannoia concurs: "Despite the best efforts of faculty committed to integration, and even trained to do so, there is only a certain amount of integrative thinking that can be taught in courses

---

26. McKenzie, "Vocation of the Christian Historian," 7.

27. Over the past couple of years there have been growing attempts to rectify the elision of Christian scholarship and Christian pedagogy, including Perry Glanzer and Nathan Alleman's parodically titled *Outrageous Idea of Christian Teaching*. However, this literature keeps intact a central proposition of the faith-scholarship paradigm in that it still sees "faith" as something that the individual teacher brings into the classroom. Both the focus on the individual as the catalyst of integration, and the assumed polarity of this flow (faith into learning) will be challenged later in this chapter.

28. Jacobsen and Jacobsen, "More Than the 'Integration' of Faith and Learning," in Jacobsen and Jacobsen, eds., *Scholarship and Christian Faith*, 27

29. David L. Weeks and Donald G. Isaak, "A Coda on Faith, Learning, and Scholarly Rigor," in Joeckel and Chesnes, eds., *Christian College Phenomenon*, 64.

designed primarily to prepare graduates for professional work or further study."³⁰

The third and final point that limits the usefulness of this type of literature to sustaining a distinctly Christian pedagogy is that the presuppositional model itself is more often asserted than proven even in the realm of scholarship where it might be presumed to be most salient. As Ronald Wells (a former Calvin College professor very sympathetic to the idea of faith and learning) observed: "Show me the books . . . I see a lot of assertions [about Christian scholarship], but I don't see much material. If you mean [George] Marsden, if you mean [Nathan] Hatch, if you mean [Mark] Noll, well sure, I know those guys; they're wonderful scholars, but there isn't anything uniquely or particularly Christian about them."³¹ Carl Trueman puts the case in characteristically provocative style. "When it comes to evangelical scholars and scholarship . . . the scandal is not that there is no [evangelical] mind; it is that these days there is precious little evangel."³² If George Marsden's scholarship is not so outrageously Christian after all, what hope for the freshman composition class?

I am not arguing that the kind of meta-level, first-order questions raised in discussions about Christian scholarship could *never* be relevant to a certain type of class (perhaps upper-level classes focused particularly on methodological issues), nor that they might not help the individual professor think about the underlying presumptions or approach of their discipline and that this might have some effect on their overall philosophy or approach to teaching. However, they are insufficient to sustain a regular, daily attempt at making the large bulk of undergraduate teaching distinctly or observably "Christian". Even in disciplines where they seem to be most relevant, they aim too high.

Worldview

My skepticism about the possibility of teaching sundry subjects in distinctly Christian ways might lead some to suggest I have not properly absorbed the idea of *worldview* as the key mediating tool to link Christianity with academic disciplines. The term "worldview" is used with a degree of definitional imprecision in the rhetoric of Evangelical education. Sometimes

---

30. Mannoia "Christian Higher Education," 104.
31. Yerxa, "Embarrassing Dream," 57
32. Trueman, "Real Scandal."

it signals the Kuyperian approach described in the previous section in which the "presuppositions" upon which academic disciplines are built are to be reconstructed according to a Christian worldview. However, many advocates of worldview (including, as noted in the previous chapter, Arthur Holmes) have seen worldview less as the *starting point* for knowledge and more as the summative *goal* toward which all knowledge is leading. Thus, according to David Naugle, Christian worldview is a vision which embraces "the holistic nature, cosmic dimensions and universal applications of the faith."[33] Nineteenth-century Scottish theologian James Orr similarly described worldview as "the widest view which the mind can take of things in the effort to grasp them together as a whole."[34]

As argued above, the concept of teaching *from* a Christian worldview, understood in the way that Kuyperians like Marsden define it, is very difficult to achieve within the constraints of undergraduate education, other than perhaps in a handful of philosophically oriented disciplines. This means that what Evangelical educators often mean when they say they are "teaching from a Christian worldview" is something much looser than the first-order epistemological and ontological reappraisal of disciplinary knowledge to which dedicated Kuyperians aspire. Rather they construe the idea of teaching from a Christian worldview to mean something like "saying something Christian about the subject at hand"—the approach illustrated in the examples from graphic design and business quoted earlier in this chapter. This approach—which may well be the best you can hope for when laboring under a pressure to teach many topics "from a Christian worldview"—tends toward the *ad hoc* and *ad hominem* attempts at tethering the subject to something biblical that were described earlier in this chapter.

The second construal of worldview as that to which one moves toward—the *telos* not just the premise of education—is potentially more useful for undergraduate education because rather than engaging in presuppositional methodological questions about epistemology and ontology (or inviting a shallow imitation of such engagement), it invites students to glean knowledge of God and the world from a range of studies and combine these into a coherent Christian vision of reality. However, as noted in the previous chapter, this capacious, holistic, and integrative project—noble and inspiring when expressed in the written literature—is difficult

33. David Naugle, "Worldview," in Bonzo and Stevens, eds., *After Worldview*, 6.
34. Orr, *Christian View of God and the World*, 15.

to sustain in the often fragmented and atomized structures of the actual Evangelical college, which often lacks any structural aids to integration.

Indeed, to achieve this ambition of graduating students who have developed a Christian view of all things, the Evangelical college really ought to ask: what are the things that Christians need to know to develop, sustain and live within such a comprehensive view of everything? It rarely asks this. Instead, it defers to typical disciplinary and professional boundaries, invites students into one or two of them (with a taster platter of others in the general education requirements, of which more below), then charges individual faculty to teach *these* subjects "from a Christian worldview." This shift from a teleological ideal of worldview being that which *puts all the pieces of life and faith together in a holistic unity* to *teaching individual classes and topics from a Christian perspective* means that students might get the *opposite* of that to which those who have championed this holistic vision of worldview aspire. Rather than seeing the whole, students at best learn how to see the parts. Yet as William Hasker observed in his classic summary of faith-learning integration: "For each of us simply to 'do her own thing' in her own classroom with her own disciplines, and leave the students to put the pieces together, will not get the job done."[35]

One can see the distinction between ideal and reality by comparing the approach to worldview taken in the average Evangelical college with the *Christian Worldview Handbook*, a volume of essays edited by one of the leading proponents of the integration of faith and learning, David Dockery. This volume promises to help readers develop a Christian worldview on one hundred topics—capitalism, art, democracy, race, war, and "every subject under the sun," as one of the endorsers puts it.[36] The *Handbook* organizes its delineation of the implications of worldview by considering crosscutting interdisciplinary themes. Without commenting on the actual arguments of the book, it is nevertheless in many ways a model for how one might help engage students with a panoramic array of vital social, cultural, economic, and political issues, all set in conversation with biblical theology.

However, the Evangelical college rarely orders a curriculum in such a way. There are not classes on the Christian view of capitalism, democracy, race, war and "every subject under the sun." Indeed, there is often no attempt by Evangelical colleges at either identifying, mapping, or addressing perennial, theological, ecclesial, contemporary, global, ethical, religious,

---

35. Hasker, "Faith-Learning Integration," 246.
36. Dockery, ed., *Faith and Learning*.

and civic issues in any kind of coherent and systematic way at all. Despite promising a Christian worldview, the Evangelical college does not actually have a concrete vision of exactly what it is about the world that Christian students ought to develop a view. Instead, students are funneled into a range of constricted disciplinary and professional fields where they dwell for a considerable amount of their time in college, often leaving vast tracts of social, cultural, civic, and theological reality unmapped and unclaimed for Christ. Moreover, by deferring to these disciplinary boundaries, students in different departments and programs might receive completely different versions of the Christian worldviews altogether. A business major might learn that free market economics are biblical; a philosophy student that free market capitalism invites serious biblical critique. A student taking classes in both departments will be left adrift.

General education requirements might be presumed to address this demand for a more unified, wide-ranging, coherent presentation of a Christian view of the world. However, the evidence that general education achieves this is meager. Critics have noted a lack of coherence of the general education curriculum at Christian colleges.[37] Cynthia Wells has described the "astonishing ambiguity as to why or whether general education matters" across American higher education and argues that Christian colleges are no exception.[38] V. James Mannoia laments the "haphazard" nature of the Christian college general education program.[39] Perry Glanzer has made a similar observation. Noting the thinness of secular universities' justifications for general education Glanzer argues that, while Christian colleges *could* offer something truly distinctive, "the reality is that Christian educators have not provided a better and more redemptive structure for general education. Christian general education by and large takes what I call the Christ-added approach to general education. In structure, it imitates secular universities that simply attempt to supply a random set of intellectual tools and skills."[40] Institutional demands to make classes flexible, transferable, and convertible between modalities, along with the growing use of adjuncts, all count against the kind of coherent, planned, integrated general education program needed to truly sustain a "holistic view of all things" worldview model.

37. Fant, *Liberal Arts*, 28.
38. Wells, "Renewing Our Shared Purpose," 58.
39. Mannoia, *Christian Liberal Arts*, 134.
40. Glanzer, "Secular University's Problematic Justifications."

The Disintegration of Faith and Learning

This tendency to atomization and lack of curricular integration may be also much less likely than the more holistic and exploratory model of worldview formation to cause any kind of controversy, and so may be preferred by administrators worried by offending key stakeholders. A cross-curricular attempt at wrestling with big issues—nationalism, race, capitalism, politics—from a Christian worldview could be explosive. It is much safer to let individual professors make small (and often platitudinous) links between the subject and the Bible. Even if a professor goes rogue, they can easily be isolated and shut down. Furthermore, the more open-ended, incremental vision of worldview is too slow and uncertain for universities that want to guard against perceptions of doubt or declension, and who desire to be able to "prove"—in specific and tangible ways—how, when, and where the "Christian worldview" has been instantiated in the classroom. As John Hawthorne has noted, a regnant paradigm of Evangelical education is that of a "factory" in which faculty are assumed to be working on an assembly line, bolting on Christianity to students who pass through their classes so that they can graduate ready to impact the world for Jesus. "Maintaining the quality means of production is done by ongoing scrutiny of faculty to make sure they don't vary from the desired qualities."[41] This approach favors a model in which worldview becomes a thing to be "added" to the student's education in a standardized and regulated way, rather than construed as an open-ended journey toward intellectual and spiritual wholeness in which both student and professor have agency and liberty.

Indeed, the regnant model of worldview integration tends to see "worldview" as a predetermined package of theological or philosophical certainties. The *nature and content* of the Christian worldview is already defined (by the administration or institutional theological guardians) and the job of the faculty is to apply it to their discipline, allowing the administration to collect "proof" of the institution's orthodoxy of the faculty to assure donors, stakeholders, and parents. This idea of a ready-baked worldview can generate a belief that there is *one* Christian worldview, and that the job of faculty is simply to announce this worldview at the right moment in their class. However, if this is so, then how is worldview different to a creed or confession? The answer, as most advocates of worldview will explain, is that worldview has *more to say* about *different and specific* aspects of life—theories of knowledge, morality, society, economics, ethics, family, law—than a creed or doctrinal confession. Yet in a model in which

---

41. Hawthorne, "Three Problematic Metaphors."

"worldview" is assumed to be already been defined, the temptation will be to *creedalize* those *specific* applications of the worldview, so that it will be assumed that a Christian worldview will inevitably issue in a certain set of political, cultural, economic, and social postures that faculty will draw on in making adjudications about particular topics. Many treatments of worldview in popular Evangelical ministries and websites make this assumption, but it is not absent from academic statements of the concept. In this way, the promotion of a putatively "Christian worldview" can become a subtle agent of secularization by importing into Evangelical colleges a suite of culturally conditioned political, economic, and social views that ought to be challenged and critiqued rather than inscribed into the fabric of the educational process.

HOW SHOULD WE THEN INTEGRATE?

Underlying the problems with the current construal of how faith and learning are brought together in the Evangelical college are two dominant assumptions so widely held that they are rarely felt in need of explanation or justification. The two assumptions concern, first, *who* is responsible for faith-learning integration and, second, how we picture *what* is going on when we envision the relationship between Christianity and education. Dislodging the hegemony of these two presumptions is necessary if we are to plot a pathway toward a different vision of Evangelical higher education.

Who Is Responsible for the Integration of Faith and Learning?

Integrating faith and learning is a bedrock contractual obligation for instructors at Evangelical colleges. Faculty must "report to department chairs, deans, provosts, and the university committees that assess whether to grant promotion or tenure; they should be able to articulate the difference and their own success at realizing it."[42] As Constance Chibuzo Nwosu summarized in her field study of the practice of faith-learning integration: "Administrators in Christian colleges and universities expect faith-learning integration to occur in the classrooms."[43] Integration is therefore nearly always pictured as something done by the singular act of the individual

---

42. Allen and Badley, *Faith and Learning*, 13–14. Emphasis added.
43. Nwosu, "Integration," 2

professor in the context of their pedagogy. Crystal L. Downing has observed that "the very word 'integration' . . . reflects modernist sensibilities, valorizing the autonomy of the individual, who within himself melds faith and scholarship into a unified, almost monumental, form."[44]

This conceptualization of integration as an act performed by a professor, bounded in time and space, can even lead to the belief that it is something one can plan for on a regular schedule and tell others when it is going to happen.[45] Constance Chibuzo Nwosu quoted one professor who claimed proudly that "she integrated three times a week." Aware that she was a subject of a study on faith and learning, this professor even apologized to Nwosu for "not integrating today" and promised Nwosu that she would "integrate tomorrow." In this discourse "integrating" is portrayed as akin to exercising or meditating—something that one can plan to occur on a regular schedule. This assumption of the highly individualized nature of professorial integration and the sense that it is primarily an act bounded in space and time has spawned detailed sociological research, such as that by Kaul et al., which "attempted to replicate Lyon et al.'s logistic regression model predicting faculty integration of faith and learning" and thus proposed the following algebraic expression that purports to predict the likelihood that an individual faculty member will "integrate."

> Logistic regression models transform the dichotomous outcome variable to log odds. If p is the probability of being an integrationist, then the odds of being an integrationist are:
>
> where $\ln()$ is the natural logarithm . . . This formula results in the logistic regression equation
>
> where e is a random error term, b_0 is the intercept, b_1 are the k regression coefficients, and X_1 are the k *predictor variables*. The estimated regression coefficients from Equation 3 can be difficult to interpret. One way to make them easier to understand is to apply the inverse of the logarithm once the parameters are estimated. The inverse of the logarithm function is the exponentiation function. Exponentiating the b_1 in Equation 3 places them in an odds ration (OR) metric. For our study, the OR represents the ration of

---

44. Downing, "Imbricating Faith," 40.
45. Allen and Badley, *Faith and Learning*, 162.

being an integrationist in one condition to the odds of being an integrationist in another condition.[46]

This belief that the act of integration can be mathematically predicted is the logical conclusion of a vision of integration that is highly observable, quantifiable, and sensate.

The assumption about the role played by the individual professor in achieving faith-learning integration is not limited to one model of Christian pedagogy. It is as evident in the more recent "embodied presence" or "incarnational" model as it is in the traditional worldview or Christian perspectival paradigms.[47] While these revisionist models stretch the notion of integration to become a more slow-burn, long-term, and relational phenomena—not necessarily something "planned" for tomorrow at 2:50 pm—they also heighten the role of the individual as ethical and faith-filled role model since they still presume that the professor is the agent who transforms the learning experience with faith.

The hegemony of this conceptualization probably rests on the tendency, noted above, to elide discussions of Christian *scholarship* with conversations about Christian *pedagogy*. Scholarship is, of course, generally the work of single individuals. It is logical that, when thinking about the viability of Christian scholarship, the burden of melding faith and learning might be seen to rest with solitary scholar, who is often pictured as blazing a lonely trail of faith in the secular academy. However, the relevance of this model to the Christian college is debatable, not least because the Christian professor working at an Evangelical college is *not* an isolated figure championing faith in the faithless academy. At an Evangelical college *everyone* is Christian, and the institution is constitutionally devoted to a Christian mission. In this very different context, it might be presumed that the burden for Christian education should be owned *jointly and collectively* by the faculty, rather than simply devolving to the heroic act of the individual. Moreover, the "product" generated by a Christian professor is not the same as that created by a Christian scholar. The work to be done is in the lives of students, not in the art of scholarly argument. Moreover, students are not readers engaging with just one scholarly work. They move through a sequence of academic experiences and interact with many Christian faculty. This fact would behoove faculty to develop a corporate, structural, and

---

46. Kaul et al., "Predicting," 178.
47. Allen and Badley, *Faith and Learning*, 62.

campus-wide notion of integration rather than devolving it to each faculty singularly.

These observations mean that although the idea that faith and learning is the responsibility of the individual faculty member is deeply ingrained in the mindset of Evangelical educators, it is not, in fact, the only way to imagine things. Indeed, there are a group of Christian educators who often work closely alongside professors in undergraduate education to whom the question of integrating faith and learning makes little sense: namely, those who work in seminaries. Of course, a seminary will want to hire faculty who wholeheartedly confess the faith that they teach, but the question of whether seminary professors integrate faith and learning is not common because the entire curriculum is organized around helping students understand and live into their faith. Faith and learning are integrated at the programmatic level, in both the content and the objective of the degree. It is not therefore up to the individual faculty to transmogrify the content, even though of course good teaching always relies on the vitality and ability of the teacher.

The question for Evangelical undergraduate education is whether it might be possible to create *programs* that are intrinsically integrative to such a degree that it would be impossible to avoid the academic content connecting with something that is bound to Christian faith and practice and which are directed toward an explicitly Christian end. In such a paradigm it would be the *institution as a whole*, not the individual faculty member, which carried the responsibility for integrating faith and learning. As is the case with a seminary, an undergraduate institution would of course want to employ individuals of deep faith and pedagogical skill, but they would be employed to deliver a curriculum which had been consciously molded around theological and missiological priorities prior to the faculty being charged with delivering a Christian education. As D. L. Hart has observed, one cannot simply take the same range of disciplines and then try to correct the way they are studied and taught in light of Christian epistemology. Rather, "a truly Christian perspective on academics might conceivably issue in universities like those in the Middle Ages or, closer to home, in nineteenth century Protestant denominational colleges, places where the curriculum and research were markedly different from the modern university's."[48]

---

48. Hart, "Christian Scholars," 396.

I am going to argue in chapter 5 that such a vision of an entirely different curriculum is not only possible but that it is, in fact, the way to overcome the secularization of the Evangelical college. The current model in which the Evangelical college offers the same classes as elsewhere, but then asks individual faculty to teach them from a Christian perspective, invites idiosyncratic presentations of Christianity and the Bible and parcels out the gospel into episodic fragments that do not necessarily ever expose students to the Christian faith in a coherent or holistic form. In resting the integration of faith and learning on the shoulders of individual faculty, faith itself disintegrates into a patchwork of observations, commentaries, and attempted correlations with the subject at hand. It also absolves the institution *as a whole* from responsibility for doing the very thing which it purports to be championing: seeing reality from a Christian perspective. The administration can proceed on largely secular grounds, adding and cutting programs according to market dictates, firing faculty and hiring adjuncts, without ever having to think Christianly about the overall curriculum.

The Unipolarity of Faith and Learning

Picturing the individual faculty member as the catalyst that transmogrifies regular learning into faith-filled education is connected to a second assumption at play in conceptualizations of Evangelical education. The question at stake in all discussions of faith and learning is "in what ways might Christian faith enliven, inform and enrich learning?"[49] There is an implicit polarity here. Faith is added to learning. Learning is rarely pictured as flowing back to inform, enrich, or reshape faith.[50] As Douglas Jacobsen and Rhonda Jacobsen observe, it is widely believed that "faith has the right, and indeed the duty, to critique learning but that learning has no authority to critique faith."[51] Faculty feel this assumed one-directional current intuitively. A professor interviewed by Constance Chibuzo Nwosu concluded that "whenever there is a problem between faith and learning . . . the problem is with learning and not with faith."[52]

49. Mark R. Schwehn, "Faith Seeking Understanding," in John Fea et al., eds., *Confessing History*, 23.

50. Hasker, "Faith-Learning Integration," 244–6.

51. Douglas Jacobsen and Rhonda Hustedt Jacobsen, "More Than the 'Integration' of Faith and Learning," in Jacobsen and Jacobsen, eds., *Scholarship and Christian Faith*, 23

52. Nwosu, "Integration of Faith and Learning," 54.

The Disintegration of Faith and Learning

There are powerful reasons for the hegemony of this way of picturing faith and learning. In part it reflects a recessive gene in the Christian college. Many Evangelical higher institutions were shaped by the early twentieth century popular Protestant movement generically known as "Fundamentalism." Fundamentalism was defined by its militant resistance to theological modernism, which was itself undergirded by nascent academic theories in both the natural and human sciences. Some Evangelical colleges were founded to be bastions of Fundamentalism, while others participated in the ethos and outlook of the Fundamentalist movement, even if they did not originate as part of that movement. Many modern Evangelical colleges are therefore heirs to a tradition that conceptualized Christian colleges as safe spaces in which the doors were firmly closed against the inroad of progressivism and liberalism that pervaded the American secular academy in the early twentieth century. Many of the issues at stake in this era related to ways in which academic approaches to the Bible, church history, doctrine, and science were challenging the authority, reliability, and veracity of central Christian doctrines. It was the liberals who wanted learning to affect faith, and the Fundamentalists who saw the acidic theories of theological modernists (many with professorial positions at leading universities) corroding traditional Christian doctrine.

On the one hand, Evangelical colleges have shifted away from the reactionary and defensive posture. The development of the modern Christian liberal arts project in the late half of the twentieth century reflected a desire for a more capacious and less suspicious dialogue with modern scholarship. Indeed, some of the earliest authors of visions about faith and learning allowed for the possibility that learning might refine and even force a reappraisal of the tenets of faith.[53] Frank Gaebelein, a pioneer of modern faith-learning integration, abandoned young earth creationism when confronted with carbon dating.[54]

On the other hand, an openness to such reverse osmosis was always a minority report and, if anything, it has receded from the discourse on faith and learning over recent decades. This reflects right-ward shift of Evangelicalism since the 1980s and a growing sense among White Evangelicals that there are dark forces at work in culture which are inimical to Christianity, many of which are assumed to be stalking the campuses of secular

---

53. Jacobsen and Jacobsen, "More Than the 'Integration' of Faith and Learning," in Jacobsen and Jacobsen, eds., *Scholarship and Christian Faith*, 20–7.

54. Beck, "All Truth," 135.

universities. A new Fundamentalism—fed by right-wing political rhetoric—is pushing Evangelical colleges back toward a defensive, reactionary posture, especially toward mainstream educational institutions. One can therefore still find rhetoric that implies that mainstream universities are "Maoist training camps engaged in indoctrination and mind control."[55] More pragmatically, the basic value-proposition of the Evangelical college in an ever increasingly competitive higher education marketplace is premised on a soft suspicion of mainstream colleges. If the secular university down the road was not in some sense deficient regarding protecting and nurturing students' faith, there would really be no need for the Evangelical college to exist.

Meanwhile discussions of Christian scholarship have entrenched the uni-polarity of faith and learning by organizing their inquiry around the question of how Christian foundations might challenge the presuppositions of non-Christian epistemologies and disciplinary methodologies. Such discussions present an image of the "secular" academy as inimical to faith and of the Christian intellectual as an outsider involved in a somewhat perilous business of poking a Christian head above the parapets of secular ivory towers. As Joel Carpenter observed, "Bringing one's religious faith to bear on the assumptions, methodologies, and structures that govern academic work is rather risky in our setting, especially if one's faith is traditional Christianity."[56]

However, as is the case regarding the individualistic notions of faith and learning integration discussed above, this widely held assumption about the directional flow of faith into learning is not the only way to see things. The idea that the characteristic which makes an Evangelical college distinctive is *faith* is reasonable if one compares the Christian college to other institutions of higher education. Yet what if one did not contrast Christian colleges with other colleges and universities but instead compared them to other Christian communities—with churches, parachurch agencies, NGOs, mission boards, and so on? Then the distinctive element of the Christian college would not be faith but *learning*. The Evangelical college would become unusual not because it injects faith into learning, but because it is the one of the only places in which the church—the community

---

55. David Hoekema, "What is Freedom For?," in Joeckel and Chesnes, eds., *Christian College Phenomenon*, 191. Hoekema was being deliberately hyperbolic in characterizing the Christian suspicion of mainstream universities like this, but the basic point he was making was serious.

56. Carpenter, "Response," 273.

The Disintegration of Faith and Learning

of the faithful who are called, saved, empowered by the faithfulness of God in Christ—studies, thinks, and learns together.

Viewing the Christian college primarily as an ecclesial institution with a mandate to educate Christians, rather than as an academic institution with a mandate to Christianize learning, changes the nature of discussions about faith and learning. In particular, this view renders redundant the tendency to portray faith as an unusual or distinctive addition to education. The concept of Christian scholarship might be outrageous in the secular guild but in a Christian institution it is anodyne. The primary community at an Evangelical college is not a group of "secular" academics but a group of (at least nominally) Christian undergraduates. The community to which one is called to educate is not a community hostile to faith. Although students will be at different levels of faith maturity there is no shortage of a visceral sympathy for a "Christian perspective" in the average Evangelical classroom. Even the closet sceptics may have learned that is what one *should* publicly profess at a Christian college. The secular, humanist, agnostic, materialist worldviews that haunt the imagination of those who wish to stress the distinctive nature of the Christian educational enterprise are chimeras in the Evangelical college community itself.

What *is* outrageous at the Evangelical college is not faith but *learning*. If "faith" doesn't get a hearing in the mainstream academy it could even be argued that opposite is the problem in the Christian college. There may be *too much* of a reflexive "Christian" perspective in the average Evangelical college classroom. There is often an instinctive desire to spiritualize complex issues, or to give the "right" Christian answer, and too little willingness to subject one's own Christian tradition to rigorous scrutiny. Ironically, in a complete inversion of the assumptions about Christian scholarship in the secular academy, the Christian pedagogue may find herself in the curious position of having to damp down the putatively "Christian" responses to questions given by students and perhaps, sometimes, even those proffered by administration and other faculty.

The tendency to frame debates about the distinctiveness of Christian academic work in light of the protocols of the academy (where one will emphasize *faith* as the distinctive element) rather than the church (where one would emphasize *learning* as the distinctive element) is unintentionally revealed in Joel Carpenter's comment (quoted above) about Christian scholarship beings "risky" in "our context." When he wrote that sentence, he was provost at Calvin College. Was it risky to be a Christian academic in *that* context?! Of course not. Carpenter was simply echoing the common habit of understanding Christian education as a subset of the academy rather than a subset of the church. Of course, there *is* a riskiness of doing education in an Evangelical community, but it is of an entirely different nature to the "risk" of being a Christian academic in the mainstream university. The Christian academic who reveals their hand in the secular university might risk being seen as a fanatic God-botherer who is trampling on the protocols of objectivism and proper scholarly methodology. But the Christian professor in the Evangelical college who uses their scholarly discipline to challenge the cultural captivity of inherited faith traditions will be viewed as an iconoclast who wishes to trample on the deeply held pieties and spiritual zeal of the institution and its members. Standing in the gap between faith and learning is more difficult when one is trying to get the faithful to learn than when one is trying to get the learned to attend to faith. Doing the latter might lead your colleagues to question your application for tenure; doing the former might lead your students to question your salvation. Contrary to assertions that the secular guild is a tough place for a believer to work, it is possible that it is in fact the *Christian college* that is the most difficult place for an Evangelical scholar-teacher to pursue their vocation.

The riskiness and challenge of educating Evangelicals *as Evangelicals* is rarely noted or discussed. This is because Evangelical Christianity is presumed to be the solution not the problem. Evangelical colleges generally see their role as *redeeming learning* (or, in the Christian scholarship discourse, *redeeming scholarship*) or, in the bolder visions of presidents and boards, redeeming culture and society. They promise a transformation of education or culture by Christianity when they should really be promising a transformation of the church by education. For example, the CCCU offers an annual networking grant for scholarly projects, but the terms of the grant only allow it to be used for projects that will bring Christian voices into the mainstream academy. The grant explicitly excludes projects that only interact with Christian communities.[57] How strange that the organization which promotes Christ-centered education does not fund academic projects that benefit Christian communities!

I am going to argue that it is by *inverting* the polarized current—by talking about learning transforming faith, not faith transforming faith—that we find a route out of the scandal of the Evangelical college. The proposal will, by necessity, also mean changing the burden of responsibility

---

57. CCCU, "Networking Grants."

The Disintegration of Faith and Learning

of delivering a Christian education from the individual to the institution as a whole. At first glance this proposal to switch the polarity will sound like I am downplaying faith in favor of learning. Everything in the Evangelical protests such a proposal. It sounds like I am elevating head over heart, earthly knowledge over spiritual wisdom, book learning against spiritual vitality, and human reason over the word of God. Isn't my plan the high road to exactly the kind of too-clever-by-half humanist attacks on Christianity that began in the universities of the late nineteenth century and caused exactly the kind of secularization of the academy that Christian colleges are determined to resist?

Such an objection is premised on an assumption that all is well with Evangelical education, and with Evangelical Christianity as a whole, and that anything that asks it to change must therefore represent a force of declension and apostasy. But Evangelical education is *already* secularized. It doesn't need any help from me. My proposal is not intended to undermine an otherwise pristine faith. It is made to liberate Evangelical education from its *existing* secularization so that it can be more fully Evangelical.

In proposing that the Evangelical college starts to think about bringing learning into faith, I am also arguing for a reorientation of the mission of the Evangelical college so that it can more consciously serve the Evangelical community. In this sense, I am also arguing for the integration of learning with the *community of faith*. Here again my argument is premised on the belief that North American Evangelicalism is not a pristine manifestation of orthodox Christianity, but a culturally conditioned ecclesial tradition that has much to learn. Such reform is currently inhibited by the Evangelical college only ever thinking about faith transforming learning. Not only does this paradigm squander an opportunity to educate Evangelicals, but it also actually tends to *import, privilege, and ossify* some of the problems with the Evangelical Christian church at large that it ought to be challenging and reforming. By imagining that faith is the shared family trait of the Evangelical college, the common factor that makes *us* unlike *them*, and by consistently celebrating the fact that it is *this* "faith" that makes the Evangelical college different to other higher education institutions, "faith" itself is subtly ring-fenced from any scrutiny. By relentlessly talking about faith transforming learning, the Evangelical colleges awards to its own often unexamined conceptions and expressions of faith an imperial authority that makes it impervious to question or critique.

Yet what if these faith presumptions—the faith and practice of folk Evangelicalism—are faulty? If this is the case, then by failing to properly examine the lived faith and practice of the community, the Evangelical college might protect and project that which is already a partial, parochial, and secularized understanding of that faith. The very thing that is meant to guard against secularization—the "Christianity" of the Christian college—may itself be a subtle agent of declension. In the next chapter I wish to argue that this is, indeed, the case. In fact, it is possible to argue that the one of the most powerful forces for secularization on Evangelical college campuses is not cultural Marxism, Darwinian evolution, materialism, humanism, modernism, postmodernism, or pluralistic liberalism, but American Evangelical Christianity itself.

Chapter 4

The College of the Evangelical Scandal

EVANGELICAL COLLEGES LOVE JESUS, this we know, for their websites tell us so. They promise to offer a "distinctively Christian environment"; a "Christian community of learners"; or a "learning community dedicated to spiritual vitality."[1] They are, most of all, "Christ-centered," a totemic affirmation of an ongoing religious buoyancy that distinguishes Evangelical colleges from other religious institutions that maintain a looser or more distant relationship with their confessional traditions. The "Christ" that is foregrounded on Christian college campuses is the Evangelical Christ. When Christian colleges meet for worship, articulate their common faith, host public events, describe their religious values, address their students, and think about their identity, they do so in the forms, style, and inflection of North American Evangelicalism.

Evangelicalism is a variety of Protestant Christianity that emerged in the eighteenth-century North Atlantic world. The Evangelical movement tuned the fundamental themes of the sixteenth-century Reformation to the pitch of eighteenth-century society and culture, including the growing belief that religion was a matter of individual choice and personal experience. Evangelicalism has flourished because it has transformed the potentially disastrous corrosion of culturally confessional Christianity ("Christendom")

---

1. Hannibal La-Grange, "Vision, Mission and Core Values"; Northwest University, "Mission and Values."

into that which Evangelicals have claimed to be the prerequisite for the attainment of true faith: individual liberty.

While Evangelical Christianity flows from many sources, at a sociopolitical level Evangelicalism is the result of bargain struck between North Atlantic Protestantism and the reorientation of politics, sovereignty, epistemology, and social ontology caused by the suite of attitudes often bundled under the label of "the Enlightenment." By the end of the eighteenth century Evangelicals and liberalizing political thinkers had forged a consensus: religion would become a matter for the individual, while capacious universal civic and political values would order the public, legal, and social sphere. Evangelicalism has therefore always possessed a tendency to make peace with the secularization of the public sphere by contending that spiritual vitality was to be located "in the heart" of the individual believer. John Locke, John Wesley, Thomas Jefferson, and the Virginia Baptists therefore all agreed: the only type of religion that was worth anything was one that was personally chosen.

It is this basic orientation of Evangelicalism toward inner, personal sanctity that has dominated a large amount of its spiritual culture. Evangelical piety, worship, preaching, literature, songs, and testimony are commonly oriented around the individual, and particularly around the affections. It is a religion of the individual and a religion of the heart. This, of course, means that a large amount of Evangelicalism is, in practice, in tension with the business of education. This is not just a problem about the particular beliefs that Evangelicals have historically embraced—creationism, or attitudes to human sexuality—running into conflict with the liberal academy, but rather that a basic disposition within Evangelicalism tends to privilege the affective, relational, and sentimental (in the classic meaning of the term) dimensions of faith.[2]

---

2. Brenneman, *Homespun Gospel*. As an aside, I am unsure that James K. A. Smith and David Naugle's answer to the scandal of the Christian college is quite right. Evangelicals do not have a problem with the affections or the language of love. It is true that Evangelical worship, lacking connections with the historical liturgical and sacramental architecture of the church, may not cultivate and order these affections correctly, but I am unsure that the average Evangelical college needs, in principle, to ditch critical thinking for more affection. I agree with Andy Olree when he argues: "I'm not sure which evangelicals he knows, but I am fairly certain I don't run in these exalted circles. My experience among evangelicals, for the most part, has led me to the opposite sort of conclusions about them: most of the evangelicals I know—certainly not all, but most—are generally suspicious of intellectualism and human reason, and are much more prone to persuade with, and be persuaded by, emotive appeals to the heart." Olree, "Review of

The College of the Evangelical Scandal

By privatizing religious experience, and by associating Christian faith with a distinct form of inner piety, Evangelicalism in effect endorses the secularization of society, since it vacates the public sphere. This means high levels of spiritual zeal in the Evangelical mode are not necessarily a bulwark *against* secularization; they may, in fact, be a sign that it has already happened. Martin Marty has pointed out that surprisingly few of those who have written about Evangelical higher education have absorbed that, in his classic study of the secularization of American higher education, James Burtchaell argued that *pietism* —a word that is sometimes used to describe the inward turn of Protestantism since the late seventeenth century—was one of the *causes* of secularization in the American academy, not its remedy.[3] As Burtchaell observed:

> The pietistic view . . . was that religious endeavors on campus should be focused upon the individual life of faith, as distinct from the shared labor of learning. Religion's move to the academic periphery was not so much the work of godless intellectuals as pious educators who, since the onset of pietism, had seen religion as embodied so uniquely in the personal profession of faith that it could not be seen to have a stake in social learning. Later, worship and moral behavior were easily set aside because no one could imagine they had anything to do with learning.[4]

The strong presence of an Evangelical culture on a campus might paradoxically accelerate secularization—the evacuation of the secular by the sacred, and the subsequent bifurcation of reality—because by affirming the interiority and privatization of Christianity it implicitly concedes many areas of

---

James Smith," 24.

3. This analysis uses the word *pietism* to describe a broad *inward turn* of multiple forms of Protestantism in the modern era. There is, however, a formal group of "Pietist" churches (including the Evangelical Covenant Church, the Evangelical Free Church of America, and the Church of the Brethren) with roots in northern European Lutheran and Anabaptist traditions. Recent work has suggested that this formal Pietist tradition should be treated with more nuance than might be implied by the more generalized use of the term "pietist" to describe the diffuse religious sentiment of evangelical Christianity. Some scholars from this formal Pietist tradition argue that, properly construed, the Pietist tradition can sustain a robust academic project by understanding the renewal of the heart as inseparable from the renewal of the mind and body, as well as offering a bulwark against the kind of cultural captivity that I describe in this text. See Gehrz, ed., *Pietist Vision*.

4. Burtchaell, *Dying of the Light*, 842.

life (and in the Evangelical college, many areas of the curriculum) to the sovereignty of discourses and practices not tethered to Christian theology.

Now, it is of course true that much of the drift of the voluminous literature on Evangelical higher education has sought to address this privatization of Christianity. This is the reason Christian scholars appeal to Kuyper's notion of every square inch belonging to God, or to the notion that "all truth is God's truth." Indeed, the very notion of "integrating faith and learning," fraught as it is in practice, is a symbolic protest against a purely interiorized piety that does not engage with social, cultural, and physical realities. However, in promoting this holistic understanding of the world as the central mission of the Evangelical college, most writers on Christian education are somewhat blind to the *context* in which the "integration of faith and learning" occurs—namely, a campus environment where many of the flaws of the demotic Evangelical tradition prevail and exercise imperial authority. This dominant Evangelical subcultural social ambience means that even if one rejected all that I have hitherto argued about the problems of the Evangelical *academic* project, and even if one was content that the existing conceptualization of Christian education was, in fact, perfectly sound, you would still be left with the fact that this project has to operate this cheek-by-jowl with manifestations of the very religious tradition that inhibited many students from developing an integrated Christian view of the world to begin with.

The Evangelical subculture of many campuses subsists in a range of practices that often operate independently of the academic project.[5] This autonomous sphere of activity reflects the broader fragmentation between curricular and cocurricular activities that prevails on many nonreligious campuses, although on the Evangelical campus some of this extracurricular space is filled with spiritual activities and protocols, some of which are, in fact, requirements for graduation.[6] The key venue in which subcultural Evangelicalism is articulated is corporate worship. Most Evangelical colleges have some formal "chapel" event that involves singing, prayer, and some form of sermon, talk, or address. Some colleges make attendance compulsory at a certain number of these events. Faculty are sometimes also required to attend. It is in this venue most of all that the style, spirituality,

---

5. This situation is, in fact, not unlike the late nineteenth century, an era in which "piety ... had a life of its own and was not amalgamated with a program of learning." Burtchaell, *Dying of the Light*, 30. See also Reed, "Shaping," 80, 121.

6. Glanzer et al., *Restoring the Soul*, 146–60.

and discourse of the broader Evangelical community is replicated and affirmed. The songs are usually drawn from the corpus of hymns and songs sung in most Evangelical churches, often led by musicians playing in a contemporary style.[7]

The deficiencies of Evangelical worship in general have been well documented. The weaknesses include: the tendency to overly individualistic sentiments; a concentration on some theological themes (cross, blood, atonement) over others (Trinity, resurrection, justice, cosmic restoration); a musical style that is derivative, twee, and banal; an inattention to grammar, syntax, and sense in lyrics; a paucity of poetic or imaginative imagery; a (surprising) lack of Scripture in favor of self-referential phrases of emotive response; and a tendency to value the spontaneous over the structured, which sometimes leads to the shallow and unbalanced. Worship, of course, is more than singing. More broadly, Evangelical worship is often critiqued for its tendency to elevate the individual leader or speaker, who alone extemporizes the prayers, denying the congregation a role in the "liturgy"; for an absence of attention to times and seasons; for a pragmatic, technologically driven mentality that values wires, screens, and amplification equipment but has little time for liturgical color, art, or symbol; and for an impoverished view of the sacraments.

Put all this into a college chapel and it is inevitability in tension with many values and postures encouraged by learning—complexity of thought, elegance of language, beauty of art, creativity of poetry and music, subtlety of storytelling, and careful exegesis of Scripture. The "Christianity lite" ethos in chapel counts against everything that "integration of faith and learning" is, in theory, meant to protest and correct.[8] Evangelical colleges too often offer "pop faith" as their template ecclesial life together. Indeed, in an echo of the relative paucity of interest in Bible and theology classes, the Bible can also be muted in Evangelical college chapels. "Chapel is certainly not unbiblical, but the Bible itself is not often present," noted one student, in what Rod Reed found to be a common student complaint about chapels at CCCU schools.[9]

This lack of sustained, coherent, and systematic engagement with the biblical text—in favor of thematic, topical, or *ad hoc* verses—reflects a well-diagnosed problem with Evangelical biblical illiteracy in general,

---

7. Page, *Now Let's Move into a Time of Nonsense*.
8. Kirkemo, "Point Loma," in Hughes and Adrian, eds., *Models*, 363.
9. Reed, "Shaping," 131.

even in so-called "Bible" churches. Much of White American Evangelical Christianity has adopted a therapeutic pietistic deism unmoored from the narratological or theological patterns of Scripture (some studies show Black American biblical literacy is higher).[10] As Dru Johnson argues, in some "so-called 'Bible-believing' white evangelical churches ... the sermon is basically quoting a bit of Scripture, sharing cute stories or insights from poems or books, and then the preacher tells the congregation what it all means. Rather than looking at what the Hebrew Scriptures or all of Paul or all of Jesus and the gospels say, the preacher bases conclusions on a single proof text. But since the congregation lacks Bible literacy and fluency, they have no way to reason together on current issues."[11] In my experience, this is exactly the model common at Evangelical college chapels (perhaps even more so, given the tendency to invite guest speakers who "pick a text"). There is, of course, a similarity between this approach and the piecemeal, prooftexting tendency which can appear in the classroom under the guise of integrating faith and learning.

The "cultural ambience" of Evangelicalism appears in myriad other ways on campus. Outside speakers—pastors, parachurch leaders, writers—may be invited to address the campus. Parachurch agencies may use the campus to host their conferences and invite students to participate. These visitors are often Evangelicals and thus communicate in the discourse of the movement, yet they are not necessarily academics and so are not participants in the attempt at realizing a holistic Christian education. An Evangelical ethos also pervades the discourse of admissions, marketing, athletics, and can even shape human resource and strategic announcements, in which God is invoked to spiritualize pay cuts, hiring and firing, and the addition or elimination of programs.

These Evangelical discourses and predilections are not just competitors with the academic project; they often trump it. Since the integration of faith and learning is such a subtle, slow-burn, nuanced thing (or, to put it more pessimistically, such a wretchedly difficult thing), it is going to be very tempting for the institution to privilege the high-octane, self-evident manifestations of religiosity (Look, parents! Here are all our students with their hands in the air worshipping God! You don't get that at the University of Statesville!) rather than showing them a carefully constructed reading list of Nicholas Wolterstorff and Mark Noll to prove their Christian credentials.

10. Nienhuis, "Problem of Evangelical Biblical Illiteracy."
11. Calvin Institute for Christian Worship, "Dru Johnson on Biblical Literacy."

The College of the Evangelical Scandal

When an institution at which I used to work built a new chapel at considerable expense, a board member told the faculty that the outlay was justified because "how can you be a Christian university without a chapel?" This statement completely undercut all the high-minded claims made in the literature of Evangelical education to the effect that learning is worship, and that the classroom is a sanctuary dedicated to holistic engagement with the truth of God's word. In this board member's construal, it turned out that faculty are not, in fact, adequately doing anything significant enough to prove that we are a Christian university after all. You also need a little spiritual brickwork visible from the highway.

In a startling example of the disconnect, I recently attended a seminar on worldview that stressed that death is not the "entry way to a better life" since this idea downplays the resurrection, a doctrine which itself helps us understand the importance of the body, and which can therefore help sustain our holistic vision of why learning about physical matters. I agree. But the next week in chapel we all blithely sang a song which proclaimed that "death is the entry way to life." In the contest of these two alternative modes of catechesis, chapel songs—emotionally piquant and melodically mnemonic—will win over readings and lectures. As the nineteenth-century English evangelical theologian R. W. Dale quipped: "Let me write the hymns of the church and I care not who writes theology."[12] Let *me* run the chapel of an Evangelical college, and I care not who teaches the classes!

In fact, the Evangelical college does not even necessarily need to overtly privilege or point to these elements of Evangelical religiosity in its quest to assert its Christian-ness. Since students from Evangelical backgrounds have been taught that authentic faith looks like the worship and discipleship experiences that they have encountered in church services, youth groups, and vacation Bible schools for their whole life, and since elements of the Christian college experience bear more than a passing resemblance to such events, then many of the nonacademic components of campus are always going to carry an inherent authority and privilege. These will naturally be seen as the carriers of true, authentic Christianity in a way that the classroom will not.

Evangelicalism magnifies this problem because its popular ethos is prone to juvenilization, sentimentality, spontaneity, simplification, and a dash of vaudeville theatrics. Such religious effervescence is always going to compare negatively to the sober, structured, routine, and complex hard

---

12. Bradley, *Abide With Me*, 81.

graft of the classroom. Students are going to tend to judge the quality of their professors' ability to bring "faith" into learning by looking only for postures that align with what they have been taught to view—and, crucially, *continue to be taught to see by the Evangelical college itself*—as signs of true Christ-centered spirituality. A professor who prays before class is probably more likely to be commended by students for integrating faith and learning than one who invites students to discuss the works of Alasdair MacIntyre for half the semester. As David L. Weeks and Donald G. Isaak observe, "In our experience, many students view any Christian activity or discussion in the classroom as pertinent expressions of the integration of faith and learning. Virtually any expression of faith in the classroom results in high evaluation marks for an instructor's faith-integration score."[13]

A tendency to privilege the ostensibly "spiritual" side of campus is manifested on the CCCU website, where it is explained that at a Christian college "the classroom and the laboratory are just as much arenas of Christian integration as the college chapel."[14] This is a revealing statement that bears deconstruction, not least because it was reading this sentence that began the whirl of thoughts which led to me writing this book. The sentence is a type of "not only but also" parallelism. It states that *not only* does Christian integration happen in the college chapel, *but it also* happens in the classroom and laboratory. Since the word *integration* means "bringing things together," and since in Christian higher education discourse the word "integration" is always a shorthand for "integration of faith and learning," what the statement seems to say is that faith and learning are not just brought together (i.e., integrated) in the chapel but also in the classroom.

But this is an odd thing to say. After all, the rhetorical punch of a "not only but also" statement relies on the assumption that the reader would be unsurprised by the first clause but intrigued by the second. My students are surprised when I tell them that King Charles III is *not only* monarch of England (which they know), *but also* sovereign of Canada (which most of them don't). Yet who would *expect* the "integration" of learning and faith to be something that happens in the chapel? Academics never happens in a chapel or a church, does it? No one would read this sentence and say, *Oh yes, I'm very used to academic things happening when we sing worship songs and pray; but I was blown away to learn that you can also bring Christian*

---

13. Weeks and Isaak, "Coda," in Joeckel and Chesnes, eds., *Christian College Phenomenon*, 65.

14. CCCU, "About."

faith into the classroom! The statement is akin to saying *you'll never believe it: Charles III is not only monarch of St. Kitts and Nevis but also of England!*

This is such an odd claim that I don't think the author of the sentence is trying to make it. Rather what has happened in this sentence is the word "integration" has become a shorthand for something like "Christian stuff." So, what that statement is really endeavoring to say is that at a Christian college *Christian stuff doesn't only happen in the chapel, it also happens in the classroom.* That certainly is the message a lot of Christian colleges try to convey. Yet by using the word "integration" to describe this scenario, the author has unintentionally revealed what they presume "integration" to be: namely, a dose of Christian stuff in the chapel and another dose of the same Christian stuff in the classroom. It this is thus a dualistic statement which, ironically, is the exact opposite of integration.

One might think I'm making somewhat heavy weather of one sentence on a website. And I would not draw such attention to it did it not cohere with the broader problem that I have been seeking to diagnose. Evangelical colleges presume that "faith" is the stable, normative, and unquestionable baseline. Faith is expressed in the chapel, and then this same faith is expressed in the classroom. At no point in this picture, though, is learning allowed out of the classroom to challenge, provoke, or interrogate "faith." In other words, to make the CCCU website statement *truly* a statement about integration, it would need to double the number of clauses. First it could indeed state (as it tries to) that Christian discipleship and worship happens not only in chapel but the classroom. But then it would also need to say (and this is the radical bit that is rarely said) *education happens not only in the classroom but also in the chapel.* This is really the far more powerful statement. It suggests that *learning makes a difference to our faith*—that the chapel and Bible study are just as much an arena of the integration of faith and learning as the classroom. As Stephen and Jane Beers observe: "When we take seriously the holistic nature of our institutions' educational missions, the student development staff and their programs become a unique and primary tool for integration."[15]

Evangelical colleges do not in fact think about integration in this holistic way. As David C. Williams has concluded, "Evangelical universities . . . do appeal to the 'whole person' but do so in a highly bifurcated fashion, with students compartmentalizing their university experience

---

15. Stephen Beers and Jane Beers, "Integration of Faith and Learning," in Beers, *Soul of a Christian University*, 70

accordingly."[16] Colleges think about Evangelical faith *changing academics*, but little about academics changing Evangelical faith, which, if it were allowed to happen, would surely begin with an infusion of learning into the very faith life of the Evangelical college community itself. While faculty are asked to bring faith into the classroom, are those responsible for spiritual activities invited to bring learning into the chapel? If not, then there is no real integration of faith and learning at all, and the dichotomization of Evangelicalism between religious and profane realms—that bargain made with modernity and secularization—has not been overcome. As Arthur Holmes realized many years ago: "The chapel program must exemplify this attitude [of integration] rather than the unthinking disjunction that is all too frequent between faith and devotion on the one hand and what goes on in the classroom on the other."[17]

While it might be tempting to view faculty as those whose high-minded integrative work is undone by the spiritual development department (an attitude that, when overheard, leads faculty to be labeled as malcontents carping from the sidelines), the reality is that the prevailing assumptions of faith-learning integration, all of which have been authored by faculty, have in part contributed to this situation. Theorists of faith-learning integration have denied themselves any basis upon which to argue against the tendency to privilege the putatively "spiritual" dimensions of the campus because, as I have already discussed at length, in the common construal of Evangelical education the main difference between a Christian and "secular" college is precisely in the higher levels of the spiritual energy present in the educational experience. This construal has had the effect of making "faith" the assumed stable, unproblematic, protected thing which is then applied to redeem a discipline, reorient a worldview, or rescue a profession.[18] Inevi-

---

16. David C. Williams, "Pietism and Faith-Learning Integration in the Evangelical University," in Gehrz, ed., *Pietist Vision*, 37. Williams argues that this bifurcation reflects the "unstable compound" of evangelicalism, divided between its Reformed wing (which influences academics) and its Pietist wing (which influences Student Development). I concur with this analysis to a point, although, as I have argued, while the Reformed wing dominates the *orization* of faith and learning, I am not convinced that it exercises dominion over academics *in practice* at many Evangelical colleges. Indeed, I suspect that pietism might dominate both chapel *and* the classroom, not least because of the inevitable temptation to privilege piety over academics within the Evangelical ambience of the college subculture.

17. Holmes, *Idea of a Christian College*, 49. See also Reed, "Shaping" 217.

18. Moore and Woodward identify this as the true binding center of an otherwise mutating and ambiguous search for a common educational and theological center to

tably, in the campus setting, faculty with this understanding of Christian education will never feel empowered or encouraged to challenge the kind of Evangelical mores on show in places like chapel, since they will naturally assume their job is to bring some of that exact spirituality into their otherwise godless classroom. Because this is hard, for all the reasons discussed so far, faculty may feel guilty about the *lack* of spiritual integration in their classroom to the extent that they are highly unlikely to start critiquing the places like chapel where the Christian credentials of the university *do* seem to be abundantly asserted and proven.

Moreover, by so resolutely viewing faith-learning integration as an act of a single professor in the context of her classroom and discipline, the literature has refused to consider *other* venues in which faith and learning might be integrated. If one works with a presumption that integration means faith coming into learning via the work of the individual faculty member, then one is not likely to consider how learning might exit the classroom and redound to the community of faith gathered in the chapel and elsewhere on campus. Evangelical college faculty have thereby denied itself the possibility that the *faculty might* have the right to *corporately* advise, oversee, and even take ownership of the *faith formation* that occurs on campus. The prevailing conceptualization of faith and learning imprisons the individual faculty within their classrooms.

EVANGELICALISM AND AMERICAN CULTURE

So far, I have focused on what might be called the spiritual predilections of Evangelicalism—a tendency to individualism, emotion, and affective piety over critical inquiry, deep reflection, and sustained thought. But a second set of issues about Evangelicalism also needs to be addressed. These relate to the way in which the Evangelical college instantiates a suite of cultural and social attitudes that pervade American White Evangelicalism. These attitudes are intertwined with theological and spiritual beliefs and practices of Evangelical Christianity to such a degree that untangling them requires concerted and careful work. Unfortunately, rather than addressing these issues, the Evangelical college often institutionalizes them.

Seattle Pacific University. Steven Moore and William Woodward, "Clarity through Ambiguity: Transforming Tensions at Seattle Pacific University," in Hughes and Adrian, eds., *Models*, 304.

Evangelicalism stresses the individual's relationship with Christ and tends to suggest that social problems can be resolved by individual conversion, and that complex questions can be assuaged by spiritual connection with God. However, this attitude does not banish the social, cultural, political spheres; it merely leads to them being vacated. Evangelicals, as members of other political, social, and cultural networks, have always possessed a set of sociocultural postures. Indeed, ironically, it may be in the society in which Evangelicalism has become *most highly individualized* (i.e., the United States) that Evangelicals have also embraced the most outspoken theological, political, and cultural agenda.

This seems like a paradox, but it need not be. The more that religious liberty is stressed, the more that faith retreats into a hypothetical private sphere (or into voluntarily constructed subcultural communities). The greater this retreat, the more that concerted, deliberative, or coherent attitudes to the public sphere rooted in the religious and theological commitments decline. This is therefore no coherent Evangelical theology of society as one might find in Catholic social teaching. Nevertheless, given that there is a natural need to fill that vacated space with something (because humans do not stop being social, political, cultural animals) then this vacuum will become inhabited by any number of ideologies drawn from culture at large.

However, humans are not entirely inconsistent. They desire rough approximations of coherence. The cultural, political, and social attitudes adopted by American Evangelicals are plausible companions to their personal faith. Because American society and culture in general has spoken in religiously freighted terms about its own identity as a country chosen and blessed by God—because in America "meet a politician where you expected to find a priest," as Alexis de Tocqueville observed in the nineteenth century—then when Evangelicals encounter and engage with culture at large they often hear ideas, language, and values that Christians may have helped create in the first place.[19] Hearing their own words—liberty, sacrifice, family values, individual responsibility, mission, Providence—spoken back to them from within civic discourse, they naturally think of them as entirely consonant with their faith and place them easily, often unconsciously, in the space vacated by the truly religious, biblical parts of their faith.

Of course, as Christian ideas and concepts have been taken up by American society at large, these concepts have been modified and untethered from their original ecclesial, theological, and biblical context. They

---

19. Tocqueville, *Democracy in America*, 306–7.

have, in fact become secularized. New Testament freedom becomes American constitutional liberty; God's chosen people becomes America; God's eschatological drama becomes fused with American global conflicts against "evil" rival empires; sacrificial death becomes the gift of the American soldier; individual choice for Jesus is extended to individualism and choice in the market; and the church becomes the nation—"the last best hope on earth." It is these secularized Christian concepts that are then reimported back into much of White American Evangelicalism where they nestle—in formal contradiction but in discursive proximity—to the original theological concepts of which they are bastard offspring. Politicians and cultural leaders aid the process by presenting their ideology or agenda as a religious issue, draping it in code words designed to touch an Evangelical nerve. Indeed, it is arguable that religious and political ideologies have become so closely intertwined since the 1980s that it is now not even necessary to frame political or cultural issues as having religious import. White Evangelicals reflexively follow the dominant ideas of the populist right, even when no apparent theological or biblical issue is at stake.

There is abundant scholarship that explores various aspects of this suite of Evangelical cultural and political attitudes. Key ideas include an affirmation of free market capitalism; anti-statism; opposition to the New Deal-style government spending and programs; highly individualistic conceptions of rights, especially gun rights; support for the United States military (tinctured with sacral language); a belief in American exceptionalism; suspicion of, and sometimes full-scale opposition to, African American civil rights (albeit today expressed more through the embrace of policies that cloak racial prejudices in other more acceptable social attitudes or which deny the legacy of past racial injustice), and a desire to "return" America to supposedly once commonly held "Christian values," most notably on issues such abortion, prayer in schools, and human sexuality. Other issues in the mix include a suspicion of science including vaccinations and climate change; high regard for the police; a tendency to dabble in the apocalyptic as a way of conceptualizing global events; strong support for the modern State of Israel for reasons of *realpolitik* and eschatological convictions; suspicion of immigration; and hostility toward Islam. And, since 2016, over all of these has loomed Donald Trump.

These social, economic, political, and cultural beliefs intermingle so intimately with the religious predilections of Evangelicalism that many people (both Evangelicals and their critics) assume that these suites of views are the inevitable result of evangelical religious convictions. Fidelity to political and cultural orthodoxy might even seen as the most important test of whether one possesses a Christian understanding of reality. After taking one popular online diagnostic tool intended to assess the existence and extent of one's Christian worldview, Evangelical literature professor Jack Heller discovered that, according to the definition of worldview used by this organization, "a person can deny the resurrection of Christ and the existence of the Holy Spirit and still have a Christian worldview if she is politically conservative."[20] While its proponents call this bundle of attitudes *the* Christian worldview, it is more accurate to describe it as the contemporary White American Evangelical worldview, thereby signaling that it is, like all worldviews, conditioned by time, place, and social (and, in this case, ethnic) positionality.

As Heller indicates, the bundle of beliefs bracketed under the White American Evangelical worldview would typically be labeled as "conservative" values. The term "conservative" is, however, a misnomer, since many of these commitments are very modern, secular, and part of the wider Western liberal political tradition. They rest not on ancient Christian tradition but on Enlightenment, individualistic, capitalistic, and nationalistic dispositions that were birthed and grew in Western Europe and North America during the eighteenth and nineteenth centuries. Such attitudes are, in fact, component parts of what Leona Nelson astutely calls "*conservative secularization.*"[21]

When Evangelicals have been worried about secularization they have typically identified *liberal* secularization as the enemy. Under the canopy of liberal secularization can be grouped any number of ideologies presumed to be corrosive of Christian truth claims and scriptural authority—cultural and theological modernism, historical critical approaches to the Bible, Darwinian evolution, atheistic communism, and so on, through an extensive list of ideologies and cultural dispositions that have alarmed Christians for several centuries. Liberal secularization has tended to have its strident champions who have deliberately cocked a snook at historical formulations of Christian faith in the name of modernity and progress.

Conservative secularization, by contrast, hides its agenda even from its advocates, precisely because it claims to be defending rather than challenging the *status quo*. Its vocabulary is rooted in an appeal to the past, even

---

20. Heller, "Divine Diversity," 1. See also Heller, "Christian College Professor."
21. Burtchaell, *Dying of the Light*, 780.

if that past, on closer inspection, turns out to never have existed, or to be much more recent than it might at first appear (certainly much more recent than the New Testament!). It uses religious language for its own ends, cloaking its secular goods in theological garb. Conservative secularization is therefore arguably the more dangerous ideology to Evangelical Christians because it is often invisible and insidious. It is a foe posing as a friend.

James Tunstead Burtchaell argues that the modern American church has been shaped by either one or other of these versions of secularization. "The typical American needs to figure out whether she is in thrall to the (liberal) academic culture, or to the (conservative) national culture (both of which are liberal historically). For the mainline churches it has been the liberal culture; for these evangelicals it has been the conservative one."[22] Burtchaell's point is significant, since his book is typically only read as an account of how liberal secularization has eroded Christian faith in higher education. It is rarely noticed that he also argued that secularization has occurred in the Evangelical colleges that he included in his study. It is strange, for example, that George Marsden, who has no doubt read *The Dying of the Light* (since he wrote the other major book on the secularization of the American academy) so breezily exempts the Evangelical college from the threat of secularization when Burtchaell produces considerable evidence to the contrary.

It is clear that "conservative secularization" has swept across large swaths of White American Evangelicalism. Evangelical colleges, drawing on this Evangelical constituency for its donors, students, and faculty, will almost inevitably import these secular attitudes. This clearly registers in political attitudes on campus. Although there is diversity of political views on many campuses, "It is impossible not to see the close connection of Republicanism and CCCU faculty."[23] Since the Republican party is clearly the home of the suite of values—nationalism, unrestrained capitalism, militarism, and nostalgic populism—this political affiliation is clearly a key sign of the phenomenon of "conservative secularization" on Evangelical college campuses. Evangelical colleges frequently extend invitations to speakers whose notoriety is based on championing conservative politics, economics, and cultural agendas.

---

22. Burtchaell, *Dying of the Light*, 777.

23. Bettina Tate Pederson and Allyson Jule, "Are We Doomed? Why Christian Colleges Must Lead on the Issue of Gender Equity and Why They Don't," in Joeckel and Chesnes, eds., *Christian College Phenomenon*, 263.

Ironically, Evangelical colleges may have become susceptible to this conservative secularization the more that they have retreated from the hard-line Fundamentalist past that defined the early twentieth century Christian college. Ditching some of theological ballast of Fundamentalism has made them more susceptible to cultural captivity. For example, conservative Christians in the nascent early twentieth century fundamentalist movement, such as Reuben Torrey, the president of Moody Bible Institute, were so equivocal about supporting American participation in the First World War, and about patriotism in general, that some were accused of being in thrall to Germany.[24] However, as Evangelicals became more significant players in the national politics and culture from the mid-twentieth century, so they have also become more ingratiating toward the values of the modern nation and economy. In this way, much of "conservative" Evangelicalism has, in fact, taken on the characteristics of early twentieth century liberal theologians in sacralizing the American civic project as an agent of God's purposes in the world, and desiring to steer it toward Christian ends. "Every time we hear the voice of the Christian nationalist, or the claims, implicit or direct, that God is on our side . . . we are in fact hearing the voice (unwittingly, perhaps, but unmistakably) of the Protestant liberal tradition," observes Charles Marsh. "When the conservative religious elites speak of the Christian nation, Christian principles, Christian values, or Christian prosperity in quasi-theological language, they are standing firmly in the tradition of Protestant liberalism."[25] Inasmuch as such appeals surface in Evangelical colleges, those who make them are advancing the very theological progressivism that the Fundamentalist founders of many Evangelical colleges rallied to resist. Talk about mission drift!

Because so much of the discourse about Evangelical higher education has worried about liberal secularization it is easy to see how the suite of "conservative" attitudes has come to be endorsed as a means by which one might become culturally more engaged without becoming more socially progressive or theologically dissolute. Cultural conservatism may have been substituted for an earlier theological conservativism as the bulwark against progressive revisionism. Thus in his study of Azusa Pacific, Burtchaell found that President Cornelius Haggard, a champion of *broadening* the college into liberal arts regime away from narrow Fundamentalism, nevertheless told students that, despite giving students "freedom to wrestle

---

24. Weber, *On the Road to Armageddon*, 83–85.
25. Marsh, *Wayward Christian Soldiers*, 103, 108.

with important ideas of life" he was only interested in "speakers who are loyal Americans, not advocating civil disorder or disobedience." "Patriotically . . . we are 'squares,'" he declaimed.[26] This was just replacing one form of Fundamentalism for another.

A startling case study of this phenomenon is provided by Michael L. Yoder in an autobiographical article reflecting on being interviewed for his first faculty job in the early 1980s. Yoder had made it to the final stage of the hiring process and been invited to talk with the president of the college. The president had read his resume, and asked him a direct question: are you going to preach at my students and indoctrinate them? This sounds like the kind of scene that one imagines plays out when a Christian scholar discloses their faith at "secular" university. In fact, the institution was Wheaton College under President Hudson Armerding. The new faculty member was under interrogation because he admitted that he was a pacifist. Despite being "Christ-centered," Armerding did not want his faculty to share his views of how Jesus compelled this faculty member to orient his faith around nonviolence. "You wouldn't get up on a soapbox and preach pacifism, would you?" Armerding demanded to know of him.[27] How ironic that Armerding would worry about "indoctrination" and "preaching" of a faith position, the very concerns that a Christian would allegedly expect to find from so-called secular universities if they revealed their faith. Dispiritingly, Yoder admits that he has from that day struggled with how much of his faith he can share in the Evangelical classroom.

Although he had served in the United States Navy, and so was presumably not himself personally pacifist, it is likely that Armerding was more worried more about public controversy than he was interested in opposing pacifism as a matter of theological principle. Although faculty, staff, and administrators may lean toward the bundle of conservative secular attitudes, it is the fear of stakeholders, parents, and donors that actually drives institutions to embrace this kind of posture. As Harold Heie observes: "Because evangelicalism is largely a populist movement, evangelical Christian colleges are very sensitive to theological boundaries that appear operative among their church and alumni constituencies, especially those constituencies who send their sons and daughters—along with their tuition dollars—to study at these colleges."[28] In his study of Pepperdine

26. Burtchaell, *Dying of the Light*, 761, 777.
27. Yoder, "Classroom Advocacy?," 83–84.
28. Harold Heie, "What Can the Evangelical/Interdenominational Tradition

University, Richard Hughes noted that "Pepperdine gradually cultivated two well-defined external constituencies. On the one hand stood a church constituency whose chief concern was that Pepperdine remain faithful to the heritage of that tradition, but this constituency did not pay the bills. On the other hand stood a donor base chiefly interested in traditional American values."[29]

While a student boom in Christian higher education during the first decade of the twenty-first century helped underwrite an era of greater openness to intellectual and demographic diversity, fears about declining enrollments have pushed Evangelical colleges back toward cultural defensiveness since the late 2010s. As John Hawthorne argues: "The declining enrollments create an incentive for schools to take a hard line on Culture War issues. Perhaps by being the 'Least Woke,' they will attract a larger share of the shrinking Gen Z evangelical market."[30] For example, Samuel Joeckel, the editor of *The Christian College Phenomenon*, a collection of essays cited multiple times in this current book, was terminated from Palm Beach Atlantic for allegedly "indoctrinating" students at on the issue of racial justice, due to a parental complaint. As Joeckel observed, although he had been teaching the class for twenty years, "There is a reason why PBA is threatening me now rather than five years ago or 10 years ago . . . they are playing a role that is a part of that culture's script: a role that says, 'We do not like to have uncomfortable conversations about race.'"[31]

Some fear that academic freedom is constrained at Christian colleges.[32] However, it is perhaps not *religious* confessions that bound academic freedom at the Evangelical college. Rather, one may be hindered from Christian freedom if one's biblical views conflict with these prevailing political and cultural views of the primary conservative secular stakeholders. As one faculty member noted in response to Joeckel and Chesnes's survey of CCCU schools: "While I am free to discuss anything in the classroom I

Contribute to Christian Higher Education?" in Hughes and Adrian, eds., *Models*, 258.

29. Richard T. Hughes, "What can the Church of Christ tradition contribute to Christian higher education? Faith and learning at Pepperdine University," in Hughes and Adrian, eds., *Models*, 421.

30. Hawthorne, "Christian Colleges Are Losers in the Culture Wars." For a full discussion, see Hawthorne, *Fearless Christian University*. (Eerdmans).

31. Jaschick, "A Professor's Job."

32. For a discussion of issues of academic freedom in the Evangelical college, see Joe Ricke, "The Hesitants Among Us: The Tightrope Act of Christian Scholarship," in Joeckel and Chesnes, eds., *Christian College Phenomenon*, 153–70.

am not free to take a strong position on several politically related issues. We have freedom to discuss, but not freedom to voice dissenting opinions."[33] Speaking in the wake of his own dismissal, Joeckel affirmed this observation: "If your religious and political beliefs conform to the conservative bent of the average CCCU institution, then your faith will probably be fine; it may even grow. But if you have any religious or political beliefs to the left of your institution, then you will find yourself in an inhospitable place where it is very easy to grow disillusioned and disheartened."[34]

While some of the conservative secular culture of the Evangelical college is a pragmatic way to stop controversy from ruining the institution, it is clear that at least some institutions make a positive virtue out of these conservative secular attitudes. For example, several Evangelical colleges overtly integrate nationalism and/or militarism into campus. Wheaton College maintains a robust ROTC program called "Rolling Thunder Battalion"—a phrase that describes the mighty voice of the risen Christ in Revelation 14:2 as he judges the empires of the world for their idolatrous appropriation of the dominion that belongs only to God.[35] Wheaton College campaigned to ensure that Christians could teach in the program, apparently happy to promote service to a military unit that styles itself with a title which belongs to Christ, as long as it is done from a Christian perspective![36] Colorado Christian goes further, describing itself as a "military-focused school," a revealing parallel to their claim to be a "Christ-centered institution."[37] Meanwhile College of the Ozarks prioritizes patriotism and military training for all students. It is proud that it does not take government funding, seemingly blind to the fact that it is shilling for the Department of Defense, the largest government department in the world. MidAmerica Nazarene is another CCCU college with a dual faith: it confesses Jesus as Lord and America as the best country in the world:

> As a Christian, evangelical university we believe Jesus Christ is Lord and the final authority for our faith and our lives . . . We believe that the American form of democratic government is the finest yet achieved, and fully support its ideals. The importance of the individual, the right of all persons to achieve, and the belief in

33. Joeckel and Chesnes, eds., *Christian College Phenomenon*, 36.
34. Lyons, "When Christian Colleges Fire 'Woke' Professors."
35. Wheaton College, "Department of Military Service."
36. Shellnutt, "Can Wheaton College Require ROTC Program Be Run By Christians?"
37. Colorado Christian University, "Military."

guaranteed civil liberties are central to American heritage, and are in line with the teachings of the Bible.[38]

These colleges are not necessarily representative of all—or even the majority—of Evangelical campuses, many of which (at least officially) take a more circumspect approach to nationalism, race, and military service. However, in many places endorsement of American values usually takes on a slightly more subtle form, finding its most powerful expression in the regency of free-market capitalism. The size and popularity of business departments is the most obvious sign of this orientation. The dominance of business departments on the campus of American universities is a phenomenon which has been discussed beyond the boundaries of Evangelical higher education, since it prompts many questions about the nature and purpose of higher education in general, and about the future of the liberal arts tradition of American universities. However, Evangelical colleges face particularly pressing issues about the size of their business departments, not least because it is arguable that capitalism—perhaps more than nationalism or racial supremacy—is the most powerful, formative social, cultural, political and, of course, economic creed and practice of the United States of America.

The centrality of capitalism to the architectonics of American life and identity makes it particularly important to scrutinize any program that seeks to enable students succeed in a highly capitalist environment, since this is the enterprise likely to import the regnant secular culture into the Christian college. Tony Campolo has observed that "my visits to Christian colleges have led me to believe that there is presently little to differentiate their programs from business and economics as offered in secular institutions."[39] Even some business professors have their doubts. "What if we're graduating Utilitarians," worries Andrew C. Herrity of California Baptist University. "It was [for a long time] unimaginable to me that my Christian business school might graduate utilitarians because Utilitarianism is a way of thinking that leads to ethical failures and moral breakdowns in business . . . Today, after listening carefully to undergraduate business students for 30 months, my response is to recognize many of my students graduate as utilitarians."[40] This is a startling admission.

38. Mid-America Nazarene, "Points of Pride."

39. Anthony Campolo, "Challenge of Radical Christianity for the Christian College," in Agee and Henry, eds., *Faithful Learning*, 150.

40. Herrity, "Graduating Utilitarians?," 133.

The College of the Evangelical Scandal

One might argue that the Evangelical collegiate embrace of business is just a pragmatic response to economic realities needed to keep the college afloat: this is what students want to do, so we do it. However, as Kevin Kruse and Bethany Moreton, among others, have argued, there is a long tradition within American Evangelicalism that has promoted capitalistic business enterprise as part of a conservative defense against government intervention in the economy, and the attendant erosion of individual rights, including religious freedom.[41] Promoting free market capitalism can therefore come to be seen as part of a proper Christian "worldview." Business departments can draw upon a tradition that has sacralized capitalism. Schools such as John Brown, Pepperdine, and The King's College have deliberately cultivated intellectual centers of "Christian free enterprise" and conservative "American studies" programs, thus "grafting conservative political and economy ideas onto evangelical ones."[42] Cornerstone University even suggests that Hayekian economics is a spiritual discipline, boasting that their business department helps "students find an intellectual pursuit where they intentionally pursue Christ, and the Austrian school of thought provides that path."[43] *No one comes to the Father apart from Mises.*

While there is evidence that Evangelical colleges endorse or propagate certain secular conservative political or cultural views about which they ought to be more circumspect, it is perhaps the sin of omission rather than commission that is most problematic at Evangelical institutions. Studies of Evangelical political and cultural attitudes since the mid-2010s, particularly in relation to the high White Evangelical support given to the presidency of Donald Trump, reveal a growing radicalization of the White American Evangelical worldview. The religious-cultural agenda of the past forty years has tipped into pugilistic anger and conspiracy. As George Marsden has observed: "When Trump was able to add open hatred and resentments to the political-religious stance of 'true believers,' it crossed a line. Tribal instincts seem to have become overwhelming."[44] A large section of the White Evangelical movement adheres to Trumpist populism with a conviction and devotion akin to religious belief.[45] Such allegiance creates absolute fealty to truth claims, however tendentious, uttered by representatives of the

---

41. Kruse, *One Nation Under God*; Moreton, *To Serve God and Wal-Mart*.
42. Laats, *Fundamentalist U*, 182–83.
43. Wierenga, "Cornerstone Students Dive Deep Into Austrian Economics."
44. Whener, "Evangelical Church Is Breaking Apart."
45. Fea, *Believe Me.*

movement, and a willingness to consider physical violence as a valid response to those who challenge or threaten the movement.

Because Evangelical colleges have long tolerated and even incorporated the basic tenets of conservative secularization into their identity and even their curriculum, and because the basic paradigm of Christ-centered education generally considers the threat to come from "other" worldviews, rather than from within the Christian community itself, Evangelical colleges are ill-equipped to confront this crisis of Evangelicalism. This is ironic because many of the problems that the contemporary White American Evangelical worldview manifests are mirror images of those identified in the so-called anti-Christian, humanistic worldviews long assailed by Evangelical cultural and academic critics. We can note two in particular.

First, White American Evangelicalism faces a severe epistemological crisis in its willingness to embrace fabrications and conspiracies. Some 74 percent of White Evangelicals believe that the 2020 election was fraudulent, without any such evidence being proven in a court of law. This is in fact a much higher percentage than Republicans as a whole, suggesting that White Evangelicals are not following the partisan crowd but leading it into the abyss of epistemological relativism.[46] Meanwhile 25 percent of White Evangelicals believe in the core tenets of the QAnon conspiracy theory.[47]

Second, White American Evangelicalism appears to be willing to embrace the Nietzschean will-to-power disposition that Evangelicals have long claimed would be the logical outcome of anti-Christian humanistic worldviews. In his seminal *How Should We Then Live*, a book that has been a touchstone for conservatives wishing to mobilize Evangelicals to resist the dangers of non-Christian worldviews, Francis Schaeffer warned Christians to be on their guard "against the special sickness and threat of our age—the rise of authoritarian government? . . . Will we resist authoritarian government in all its forms regardless of the label it carries and regardless of its origin?"[48] Writing in the midst of the Cold War, Schaeffer meant this to be a warning against the rise of Communism and socialistic government policies (indeed, the paragraph from which this quote is taken implicitly critiqued Christians for being too worried about racial justice and not enough about big government). Most Evangelicals influenced by this Schaefferian mode of discourse would continue to read the warning like this, seeing this

---

46. Cox, "Rise of Conspiracies."
47. Jenkins, "Survey."
48. Schaeffer, *How Should We Then Live?*, 256.

as proof why voting for the "Woke Liberals" is dangerous. But it is hard not to spot the irony in Schaeffer's warning.

Schaffer warned that "the danger of the rise of authoritarian government is that Christians will be still as long as their own religious activities, evangelism, and life-styles are not disturbed."[49] If Schaeffer realized the danger of an authoritarian government which left people of faith to their own devices, how much more dangerous would be (and is!) the scenario in which when Christians are not just left alone, but actively flattered by an authoritarian movement that offers them access to power and privilege. "Boy do they understand me. They understand me better than anybody," noted Trump of Evangelicals.[50]

Even more dangerous would be the situation which would transpire (and has transpired!) when Christians themselves become prominent leaders of an authoritarian movement, and help the movement drape itself in the mantle of Christianity. For example, Eric Metaxas, who regularly speaks at Evangelical colleges, claims that those who do not support Trump are akin to those who would have supported the Nazis, and hints at the need for violence in support of his agenda.[51] Indeed, the Public Religion Research Institute finds that 31 percent of White American Evangelicals believe that violence may be necessary to rescue the country from its present danger. This is the highest commitment among any religious group, and higher than the national average (which is itself 23 percent).[52] White Evangelicals appear to be the leading champions of political violence in the name of a leader who most Evangelicals admit is not Christian yet is sometimes likened to Christ.[53]

An interlocutor might argue that my argument gives the liberal or progressive worldviews a pass. They would suggest that identity politics or postmodern epistemologies represent an equally authoritarian threat as they police speech or vest truth claims in subjective positionality rather than universal reason. They might point to incidents of left-leaning violence. There is no doubt much to be critiqued about liberal, progressive, or naturalistic modes of inquiry and political discourse. And perhaps it is indeed true that shadowy anarchist groups are intent on fermenting

49. Schaeffer, *How Should We Then Live?*, 256.
50. CBS Minnesota, "Trump on Evangelicals."
51. Dreher, "Eric Metaxas's American Apocalypse."
52. Slisco, "White Evangelicals."
53. Empsall, "Blasphemy."

domestic insurrection with a passion equivalent to right-wing militias. But whatever deficiencies or dangers such ideas and organizations possess, they are not the worldviews or networks to which *White American Evangelicals* are beholden. When Evangelical colleges frame their educational mission as correcting the problems of liberal progressive worldviews, they tilt at windmills located well beyond the Evangelical community itself. Certainly, if an Evangelical institution had a college full of liberal progressives, they might be warranted in aspiring to help such students see the error of their ways. But they do not have such a constituency. They have a college full of majority White American Evangelicals. The *actual* threat to Evangelical Christianity is not secular humanism, liberal progressivism, critical race theory, or Antifa. It is the creeping epistemological, moral, and political canker that comes from within the White American Evangelical movement itself.

Evangelical colleges ought to address this crisis with urgency. Instead, they ignore it. This is because they operate with a paradigm of Christian education that finds it hard to imagine how it might be *our* worldviews—not theirs—that are faulty; because challenging the White American Evangelical worldview would lead to the collapse of financial and stakeholder support; and because they define their mission toward students primarily as providing a conduit to employment, not as contributing to the moral and spiritual formation of the church.

CONCLUSION: THE OUTRAGEOUS IDEA OF EDUCATING EVANGELICALS

The White American Evangelical worldview is not the only Evangelical worldview, let alone the only Christian worldview. The question for Evangelical colleges is whether they wish to subject *this* worldview to the same kind of critical analysis as *all other* worldviews, or whether they in fact wish to reify and institutionalize it. Are Evangelical colleges primarily *nodes* of an Evangelical subculture—participants in its infrastructure, and thus invested in its success and defense? Or are they outsiders looking in, willing to subject the Evangelical world to scrutiny and critical analysis in the name of the gospel?

If we care about the spiritual, ethical, and theological health of the Evangelical community, Evangelical colleges must put critical distance between themselves and the White American Evangelical worldview. They must be sufficiently independent of Evangelicalism to be able to speak prophetic truth to it, even if doing so carries great risk. Ironically, this very critical distance from demotic Evangelical piety and cultural mores might be just what students need to *keep* the faith. As John Hawthorne observes, Evangelical colleges are often run by administrators and trustees fighting cultural battles that are remarkably out of step with the actual spiritual, moral, and academic temperament and needs of students.[54] Moreover, in regard to the prevalent Evangelical spiritual subculture, Carol Woodfin has observed, based on an empirical study, that "the Christian 'atmosphere' on campus—chapel, the numerous opportunities for Bible studies, mission trips, or other ministries—often touted as attractive by faculty, students, parents, administrators, student development officers, and outside constituencies has a surprisingly *negative* effect on the faith development of many students."[55] By refusing to critique and challenge Evangelical culture, the Evangelical college may become a stumbling block to students' faith. If this is so, it is the greatest scandal of all.

Evangelical colleges should not be "safe spaces" for Evangelical Christians. They should be places in which Evangelicals risk learning about their own identity and disordered loves and invited to refashion their understanding of Christ and his kingdom through learning to distinguish the *evangel* from modern Evangelical subculture, as well as from all other claimants to their allegiance and identity. If the Evangelical college defined its primary mission as the catechesis and renewal of the Evangelical Christian community, it could become a force for spiritual and ecclesial revival.

---

54. Hawthorne, "Christian Colleges are Losers in the Culture Wars"; Hawthorne, "On Not Fighting Culture Wars."

55. Carol Woodfin, "Faith and Campus Culture" in Joeckel and Chesnes, eds., *Christian College Phenomenon*, 91.

Chapter 5

Doing College for the People of God

WE NEED TO STOP bringing faith into learning and start bringing learning into faith, and into the community of the faithful. This vision might trigger suspicion from two sides. First, because we are so used to the idea that the way that a college proves its "Christian-ness" is to emphasize the infusion of faith into learning, then switching the formulation to talking about integrating learning with faith will sound as if I am *downplaying* the role of faith. Indeed, it might even sound as if I am advocating for exactly the kind of approach to faith that led to classic secularization in which the tenets of faith must concede to the authority of modern learning. Was it not the historical critics and modernist theologians of the early twentieth century who argued that the dogmas of faith must bow to the regency of new scientific, sociological, philosophical, historical, and literary paradigms?

I am confident that my proposal does not mean this. In fact, reversing the integrative flow accentuates rather than diminishes the importance of faith in Evangelical colleges. When we talk about bringing faith into learning, we in fact make teaching and learning the end goal of our endeavors. We have seen the consequences of this. Too often Christ comes along for the ride on what is essentially a secular project of higher education. But we want Christ, not learning, to be our goal. Faith is not the starting point of our endeavors but the end goal; our learning (and, indeed, all our endeavors) must help us know and serve Christ better. We preach Christ and him crucified, not cybersecurity and Christ integrated.

Moreover, as I argued in the previous chapter, the lived and practiced "faith" of the Evangelical community needs our sustained and concerted attention. It needs revival. Ultimately, of course, such work will be the result of the Holy Spirit bringing renewal and reformation. But the Spirit works in and through the church. The Evangelical college is a ministry of the church. If Christ-centered educators believe they are called to study and teach, they must also believe it possible that revival could come through the ministry entrusted to them—through the Spirit using their words and actions to convict, stir, and refresh the church. To the Evangelical college is entrusted a distinct ministry that no other part of the Christian church can fulfill: to nurture Christians who can think more clearly about the world and the gospel, so that they can become full participants in a church that is serving the mission of God. As George Marsden observed, the key question for Evangelical colleges is "what are we educating for . . . what kind of community are we trying to create?"[1]

The essence of the vision that I am proposing has been most cogently proposed by Douglas Jacobsen and Rhonda Jacobsen. Their formulation is imperfect because they are discussing scholars and scholarship rather than Evangelical pedagogy (a tendency we know is typical in many discussions of faith and learning). Nevertheless, their vision is worth quoting at length because, with a few tweaks, it helps clarify my proposal:

> We need education to shatter the misshapen forms into which we have molded our culture-bound expressions of faith, along with the naïve and simplistic ways in which we often imagine society at large to operate, and hence how we imagine we as Christians must live within this society. Our cognitive, affective, liturgical, and ethical expressions of faith ought to be challenged by learning, and, as this happens, the apostolic faith might be allowed to expand into areas hitherto closed off by our unquestioned cultural assumptions. Thus, the academic critique of Christian faith can actually help make Christian faith more Christian . . . Besides faith-informed scholarship . . . we also need academically-shaped faith in which Christian scholars turn the issues around and use their disciplinary knowledge as a fixed point of reference to critique or tweak their own Christian faith.[2]

---

1. Marsden, "Moving Up," in Joeckel and Chesnes, eds., *Christian College Phenomenon*, 336.

2. Douglas Jacobsen and Rhonda Hustedt Jacobsen, "Contours and Contexts of Christian Scholarship," in Jacobsen and Jacobsen, eds., *Scholarship and Christian Faith*, 154.

If we substitute the Jacobsens' emphasis on scholarship for pedagogy (i.e., if we rewrite the last sentence to read "we need academically-shaped faith in which *faculty in Evangelical colleges* turn the issues around"), then we have a startlingly radical manifesto for the Evangelical college. We do not need Christ-centered learning but learning-shaped faith. Learning-shaped faith, however, is not elitist, abstract, or esoteric faith. Rather, learning is the way to free our Christianity from the tyranny of time and place, from the captivity of culture, and from the idolatry of our age. In short, we need learning "to make the Christian faith more Christian." This should be the central and defining goal of the Evangelical college.

We can, however, go one step further. While it is certainly important to view the work of learning as helping individual students to better know Christ, the Evangelical college should aspire not just to cultivate individual students' spiritual discipleship but to revive and renew the Evangelical Christian community. The goal of learning is not just a purified "faith" in the abstract or even a mature individual faith, though both these things are important. Rather, the aim must be to teach *toward* the formation of the church. The Evangelical college must summon, catechize, and prepare the people of God for the mission of God. In the words of Michael Budde, one of the few scholars to have glimpsed this vision of the Evangelical college, the job of the Evangelical college

> is not credentialing, not job training, not turning out a "well-rounded person," not the development of the participant's human capital. The purpose . . . is to make participants more fully into disciples shaped by the priorities and practices of Jesus Christ; to help them discern their vocation as members of the transnational body of Christ; and to contribute to the mission of the church—to help the church serve more fully and faithfully as a foretaste of the promised Kingdom of God, on earth as it is in heaven.[3]

Given that I have just argued that the point of learning is to nurture and create faith, critics from the other side now might register their fear that what I am proposing will *downgrade* learning and lead Evangelical colleges to regress to a Christ-against-culture, sectarian, and doctrinally narrow version of higher education. Again, I do not think this is true. Paradoxically, when we switch polarity to make *faith* the object of our endeavors, we also *heighten* the importance of learning. It is when learning is always

---

3. Michael L. Budde, "Assessing What Doesn't Exist: Reflections on the Impact of an Ecclesially Based University," in Budde and Wright, eds., *Conflicting Allegiances*, 256.

under suspicion—always felt in need of redemption or reformation—that we are in danger of losing academic credibility and strength. We worry about teaching "ordinary" subjects, fret about whether we are teaching from a Christian worldview, try to find ways and times to "integrate," no matter how tenuous.

Focusing on the role that learning plays in maturing the faith and practice of the church is likely to produce a much stronger and more robust academic culture. This is because in this formulation it is not our *content* that makes our college Christian, but the end to which we wish this content to be used. We turn ordinary learning to redemptive, missional kingdom ends when we direct it toward the gathering, renewal, and maturing of the Christian church. We therefore do not need to feel guilty that we were trained at "secular" institutions, or use "secular" teaching materials. We do not need to apologize because our classrooms deal with regular facts and information. We do not always need to be judging the "worldviews" of the authors or individuals that we discuss. To be sure, there may be times when this is needed. But the academy is already pluriform and subject to robust internal debates about methodologies and presuppositions. We are Christian because we educate Christians to do Christian things, not because we expose or correct the faulty presuppositions of the mainstream academy.

By making the cultivation of *faith* and the *faithful* our primary task we therefore can fully embrace our calling as *educators* and champions of learning. No one else in the Evangelical community will take up this mantle. The value of learning is ours to embrace unapologetically. When we recognize that our vocation is to help God's people grow in their knowledge and understanding of God, the world in which they are called to live as agents of God's redemptive purposes, and their identity as members of a global Christian church, then we can fully embrace all the scholarly and educational tools at our disposal. We are authorized to unleash learning in the service of God. Our role as Christian educators is to promote and defend the need for robust and unashamed use of God-given critical faculties among the Evangelical Christian community. Stressing the formation of the church as our primary vision allows us to think, learn, write, and debate more confidently and unapologetically. Learning is enhanced when the cultivation of faith and the faithful is prioritized.

What would it mean to orient our Evangelical colleges around the formation of the church? What would it mean to integrate learning with faith? To work this out is the task of a generation, not a chapter. We have hardly begun to think or talk in such terms, and the whole scandal of the Evangelical college militates against the conversation even beginning. Still, we must begin somewhere. In what follows I want to first make five observations about the church that should inform how we think about the role of the Evangelical college. After this, I will sketch out some guiding principles for a new Evangelical college.

FIVE OBSERVATIONS ABOUT THE CHURCH

First, the church is a community of people united in Christ. This community therefore possesses, shares, and expresses the fullness of what Christ has achieved. The good news of Jesus Christ is the restoration of humanity as a central part of God's redemption of the whole created order. The church is not a negation of humanness but its renewal. As James K. A. Smith has argued: "The church is elected to responsibility called to be the church to and for the world—not in order to save it or conquer it to even transform it, but to serve it by showing what redeemed human community and culture look like, as modeled by the One whose cultural work led him to the cross . . . we win by losing."[4] This means that to learn to be the church also means to learn to be human. As N. T. Wright contends: "The biblical vision of being human is that of being God's Image-bearers: which means being like an angled mirror, reflecting God's wise, stewardly love into his creation. The Christian vision is of Jesus as the true image and of Jesus' followers, shaped by his Spirit, being transformed 'into the same image' (2 Cor. 3.18). Being truly Christian and being truly human ought to come to the same thing."[5]

Second, this restoration of humanity is incomplete when expressed singularly. As Stanley Grenz observes: "The image of God does not lie in the individual *per se* but in the relationality of persons in community. The relational life of the God who is triune comes to representation in the communal fellowship of participants in the new humanity."[6] Living as humans *in community* is a Gospel task. Renowned missiologist Lesslie Newbigin argued that "the intention of Jesus was not to leave . . . behind a disembodied teaching" but rather to create "a community which would continue that

---

4. Smith, *Desiring the Kingdom*, 207.
5. Wax, "Rebirth of Virtue."
6. Glanzer et al., *Restoring the Soul*, 283.

which he came from the Father to be and to do—namely to embody and to announce the presence of the reign of God."[7]

Third, the church is a *political, economic, and social* body and, as such, it subverts and rebukes other political, economic, and social realities. Rodney Clapp argues that the church is not called to "be relevant to culture but to *be* a culture."[8] In word and sacrament, the church is called to an act of subversion of all other narratives, identities, and patterns of existence. N. T. Wright argues: "A great deal of Christian theology consists of the attempt to tell this story as clearly as possible, and to allow it to subvert other ways of telling the story of the world, including those which offer themselves as would-be Christian tellings but which, upon close examination, fall short in some way or other."[9] James K. A. Smith draws a similar conclusion: "A Christian community that seeks to be a cultural force precisely by being a living example of a new humanity will have to consider abstaining from participation in some cultural practices that others consider normal."[10]

Fourth, the church is invited to be a *partner* with God in his mission. "Mission" is used in the sense deployed by a body of theologians, both Catholic and Protestant, who insist on "theological priority of *God's* mission" (commonly termed the *missio Dei*). "Fundamentally, our mission . . . means our committed participation as God's people, at God's invitation and command, in God's own mission within the history of God's world for the redemption of God's creation."[11] The mission of God is construed as the entire purposes of God toward his creation. The word "missional" can be used to describe a theology that is centered on the "dynamic significance of God's mission" and also to characterize a Christian community that takes its liturgical and ethical priorities from this all-encompassing mission of God.[12] As Christopher Wright explains, "It is not so much that God has a mission for his church in the world, but that God has a church for his mission in the world."[13] Christians are authorized by God's expansive mission agenda to construe a whole host of activities as "missional." This of course includes inviting individuals to be reconciled with God. It

---

7. Newbigin, *Gospel in a Pluralist Society*, 133–34.
8. Clapp, *Peculiar People*, 75.
9. Wright and Bird, *New Testament in Its World*, 881.
10. Smith, *Desiring the Kingdom*, 209.
11. Wright, *Mission of God*, 22–23.
12. Wright, *Mission of God*, 24.
13. Wright, *Mission of God*, 62.

also involves "reconciling between estranged enemies, restoring justice, building community, caring for the earth, ending the arms trade, growing and distributing wholesome food, providing safe and ecologically modest transport, healing bodies and minds."[14] As Lesslie Newbigin observed, "if God's elect are called out of themselves into the society of the church, then the church is called as agent of renewal for all humanity." A wide-ranging education is vital to the church, because "the fulfillment of the mission of the Church thus requires that the Church itself be changed and learn new things."[15]

Fifth, the church lives within the eschatological time inaugurated by Christ's death and resurrection. The church's call is "to live out within the present old order of the world the truths and values of the in-breaking new order of the kingdom of God."[16] It is this very eschatological life of the church that by which it fulfills its missional calling. As Newbigin puts it: "The church . . . calls men and women to repent of their false loyalty to other powers, to become believers in the one true sovereignty, and so to become corporately a sign, instrument, and foretaste of that sovereignty of the one true and living God over all nature, all nations, and all human lives."[17]

Put together, this vision of the church is holistic, universal, and dynamic. First, it is holistic inasmuch as it affirms the central proposition which writers on Evangelical education have tried to affirm for several generations: that Christianity is not just a personal or inward disposition but the story of God's involvement in the whole of creation. If creation is a restoration, not a negation, of our humanness, studies of human action, ideas, and communities must be central to any Christian education. Orienting our education around the church does not inherently narrow our curriculum—although it will probably radically change it.

Second, the vision of the church is universal inasmuch as the church is not just a voluntary society where saved individuals go to worship together; it is a community that embodies, acclaims, and acts upon the total Lordship of Christ over all things, and embodies and anticipates the present and future reign of Christ. The job of the Evangelical college must be to acculturate students, many of whom will have a partial or constrained view

---

14. Kreider, *Worship and Mission*, 54.
15. Newbigin, *Gospel in a Pluralist Society*, 124.
16. Wright, *Mission of God*, 311.
17. Newbigin, *Foolishness to the Greeks*, 124.

of "church" to the full depths and breadths of the countercultural identity the people of God. As Glanzer and Ream contend:

> One of the most obvious ways the curriculum should differ is that a Christian college or university should acknowledge that the Christian identity will be more fundamental than American or professional identities when ordering and arranging the curriculum. Such an understanding an ordering entails helping students live and think about their own stories, first and foremost, in light of Christianity's story and the community that embodies it, the Church.[18]

Finally, this vision of the church is dynamic. Christianity is not a set of propositions but an unfolding narrative of redemption. It has a beginning, middle, and end, but it also has a contingent space in which the church lives and improvises considering the past and in anticipation of the future. The dynamism of the Christian story is given by *eschatology*. Eschatology means "the doctrine of the last things." But eschatology is never just about a sequence of events that will happen at the end of time. It is about the unfolding reality of God's ultimate plan. For Christians eschatology begins at the cross and empty grave of Christ. A new age—and a new humanity—has already commenced in Jesus and the church. As Jürgen Moltman famously argued: "A proper theology would therefore have to be constructed in the light of its future goal. Eschatology should not be its end, but its beginning."[19] Eschatology thus unites past and future and opens the space in which the Christian church must live.

Eschatology is, in fact, a missing piece within thinking about Christian higher education. Rodney J. Sawatsky has noted that much of the justification for Christian education has been rooted in the doctrine of creation, the study of a world made by God and of humanity created in the image of God. He argues, however, that there needs to be a much stronger eschatological reflection on the nature, purpose, and activities of a Christian college.[20] How does this college anticipate the world that is to come? And how does it prepare students to be a part of the community of the last days—the church—that is called to anticipate and symbolize the rule and reign of God? Grounding the Evangelical college in eschatological reflection would

---

18. Glanzer and Ream, *Christianity and Moral Identity*, 195.

19. Moltmann, *Theology of Hope*, 16.

20. Rodney J. Sawatsky, "Prologue: The Virtue of Scholarly Hope," in in Jacobsen and Jacobsen, eds., *Scholarship and Christian Faith*, 19.

be a major bulwark against secularization. For example, an immersive, contextually sensitive reading of the most prominent eschatological vision of the New Testament, the book of Revelation, would probably change many of the priorities of Christian college. Revelation acts as "a kind of purging of the Christian imagination," explained Richard Bauckham, "refurbishing it with alternative visions of how the world is and will be."[21] Would it be possible to absorb Revelation's vision of empire, commerce, and power vanquished by the suffering Lamb and still argue that the Evangelical college, as community of the last days, ought to be worried about market-sensitive programs and transferable skills?

This conceptualization of Christianity as holistic, universal, and dynamic coheres with the idea of "narrative worldview," articulated by Richard Middleton and N. T. Wright. Susan VanZanten has noted that "a narrative worldview is vastly different from a foundational presuppositional worldview, yet the differences between the two are not often recognized in mission-driven institutions or the literature on Christian higher education."[22] At the basis of the idea of narrative worldview is the argument that humans are storytellers who tell stories about their origins, predicament, and destiny in order to make sense of the world and order their desires and actions. Worldviews are narratives which address the same basic set of questions: "Who are we, where are we, what is wrong, what's the solution, and what time is it?"[23]

One can, of course, "learn" the "correct" answers to these questions from a Christian point of view. The narrative arc of the Christian worldview is often described as a drama of four parts: creation, fall, redemption, and final consummation. However, the point about a narrative worldview is not that it is a static body of propositions or truth claims that one can learn and then use to adjudge different aspects of reality. Rather, it is an encapsulation of an ongoing, dynamic story. Worldview is not that *from* which we teach but the location *from within which* we teach and learn. Christian education occurs *in media res* of God's narrative arc. Thus, the narrative worldview is not something to be taught to students so that they can describe it; rather we desire that all Christians *inhabit* the Christian worldview, that is, live within God's story. If we construe the purpose of Evangelical education like this, it seems inescapable that the corollary of this ambition is that we must

---

21. Bauckham, *Theology of the Book of Revelation*, 17.
22. VanZanten, *Joining the Mission*, 121.
23. Wright, *Paul in Fresh Perspective*, 7.

teach students to live within the church, which is the body of Christ and the agent of God's mission on earth.

Indeed, it is arguable that the call to live *within* the Christian worldview (that is, within the Christian story) should be made in the first instance not the students, but to the Evangelical college itself. The Evangelical college—its administration, president, trustees—needs to learn to see *the Evangelical college* from within the Christian narrative worldview. Evangelical colleges need to ask the central worldview questions: Who are we? Where are we? What's wrong? What's the solution? What time is it? I do not mean that the Evangelical college should ask these as a kind of Christianized SWOT analysis, where the answer to "what's wrong" is something like "declining enrollments and high discount rates." I mean that the Evangelical college should use these questions to position itself within the narrative arc of God's redemptive story. The Evangelical College must learn to think of itself from a Christian worldview—and then, since the worldview is a dynamic story, it must act accordingly. Faith is not something to be integrated into the Evangelical college; the Evangelical college is something that must be integrated into the reality of God's mission toward the world.

WHAT WOULD A RENEWED EVANGELICAL COLLEGE LOOK LIKE?

A Whole New Curriculum

The Evangelical college needs to completely rewrite its curriculum. There is a strong and a weak version of this proposal. The more radical proposition is that the Evangelical college drastically simplify its entire catalog, reducing it down to just one or two majors. The main effect would be to eliminate any "practical," career-oriented program. As Arthur Holmes breezily put it: "Vocational courses are usually available to students in the summer or on a semester off. The Christian liberal arts college does not have to satisfy every such desire, and perhaps should devote its resources to what is more central to the strategy of integrated Christian liberal learning."[24] Robert Brimlow concurs: "There doesn't appear to be a need for the church to train students to be accountants, lawyers, physicians, or managers. There are fine secular institutions like Stanford, Michigan, Princeton, Notre Dame, and

---

24. Holmes, *Idea of a Christian College*, 42.

Georgetown that are quite proficient at producing corporate and civic leaders."[25] Of course, this idea will seem so odd that it is seen as risible. The whole drift of Evangelical college history over the past fifty years counts against it. And there is no doubt a huge risk in such a plan. But it is not necessarily silly. It could be prophetic.

Imagine first that the "core" or "general education" curriculum of the Evangelical college would be neither the traditional liberal arts disciplines nor skills-based classes (such as communication or math), but rather multiple classes in biblical studies and theology, and classes that help students understand their own Christian tradition within the broader context of historic global Christianity. In effect, by taking this general education "core" students would gain a major in something like "Christian studies."

For those colleges that use "worldview" language, this commitment to around forty hours of Christian studies would signal an absolute commitment to helping students develop a comprehensive and deeply grounded Christian theological groundwork as the foundation for all their subsequent studies—and, indeed, for their future life and work. This would be a much more effective way of developing a Christian worldview than trying to insert bits and pieces of Christianity into disciplinary-based majors, or even trying to tether Christian worldview to the classical liberal arts subjects As Glanzer, Perry, and Ream argue, "A Christian university general education should not simply place a couple of Bible or theology courses into the curricular mix as if that actually helps students obtain a coherent understanding of how the rest of the curriculum fits into God's story."[26] For colleges who do not use "worldview" language, this Christian studies core would be the opportunity to inculcate whichever theological, confessional, and missiological priorities shape the institution's understanding of full-orbed, holistic Christian life and action. Whether you call it "Christian worldview" or just "Christianity," the priority should be the deep immersion of students into the Bible, Christian theology, and understanding of the historically and culturally conditioned interpretative communities in which contemporary Christian beliefs and actions have been forged. In short, getting a major in Bible and theology should not be optional at an Evangelical college.

---

25. Brimlow, "Who Invited Mammon?" in Budde and Wright, eds., *Conflicting Allegiances*, 168.

26. Glanzer et al., *Restoring the Soul*, 234.

Next, at the point when students typically transition from their "general education" requirements to their disciplinary major, students in this reimagined college would commence an interdisciplinary major. The curriculum of this major would center on the question of what it means to be the church (with all the deep resonances of what "church" means that are described above) in and for the world. To answer this question, students would of course need a deep knowledge of the structures, cultures, ideologies, conflicts, politics, economics, language, and history of global, national, and civic contexts. To understand each of these contexts is the work of many disciplinary perspectives working in harmony. The curriculum would be structured thematically, not by discipline. One would also need to carefully reveal the ways in which Christian identity, belief, and practice has itself been distorted or deformed by the very structures, narratives, and ideologies that one is learning about. This proposal gels with Nicholas Wolterstorff's proposal that the Christian college needs to "walk in unchartered territory" regarding curricular offerings, eschewing the traditional streams of learning—"physics, literary criticism, music theory, economics, and so on"—in favor or "new ways of packaging learning" appropriate to Christian mission. "Perhaps we shall need programs in peace and war, nationalism, poverty, urban ugliness, ecology, crime and punishment."[27] Likewise, Glanzer et al. propose interdisciplinary "courses [that] would overcome the problems that occur by allowing general education to be dictated by subject matter boundaries. Christian colleges and universities must structure their curricula differently so that it coheres with their particular aims."[28]

Finally, after taking this double major in Christianity and the contemporary world, students would be left with around forty more credits. Here the reimagined Evangelical college could offer students a choice of in-depth, project-based, experiential, or vocation-focused classes. Some of these might be traditional "electives," in which students go deeper on topics that have piqued their interest during their prior studies. There would be opportunities for civically engaged projects, or faculty-mentored research. Domestic or overseas study experiences or acquisition of a language could also be part of these thirty-some credits.

The immediate objection to this proposal is that it fails to give students any practical skill or qualification. One might, of course, reply that the question is beside the point. If the education proposed here acculturates

---

27. Wolterstorff, *Educating for Shalom*, 34.
28. Glanzer et al., *Restoring the Soul*, 204.

a student to their identity as a member of the body of Christ in which they become full participants in the mission of God as they anticipate the kingdom of God on earth, then is it really the case that the Evangelical college can be adjudged to have failed in its mission if it has not also told them how to gain a job in middle management? This mission of the Evangelical college must focus "on developing humans made in God's image for Christ and Christ's kingdom and not merely citizens for this world or professionals for jobs."[29]

Still, one cannot be blind to reality. Students only come to the Evangelical college because our society recognizes—and the federal government subsidizes—this liminal four years of a young person's life as the period during which they gain skills to become gainfully employed. And the New Testament itself has stern warnings against those who use Christianity as an excuse not to work. Thankfully, we do not need to make the choice between receiving a genuinely Evangelical education and being able to secure an income sufficient to live. There is a large body of evidence that suggests that students do not, in fact, need career-specific training to engage in meaningful, creative, and, yes, even decent-paying, work when they leave college. Many commentators, writing from non-faith positions, affirm that value of breadth over depth: for thoughtful, critical, creative, and communicative individuals who understand multiple cultures, ideas, and perspectives. A major that immerses students in an interdisciplinary study of the foundational structures, societies, ideologies, and communities of the world is surely not at all a degree that would be seen as useless.[30]

Indeed, in following through the logic of imagining a new curriculum that invites students into broad, crosscutting global, and civic knowledge in the name of learning to be the church in the world, one might also produce a curriculum that offers an innovative interdisciplinary major that could, in fact, be a model for curricula transformation, even at non-Christian institutions. Could it be that, by abandoning the attempt to replicate secular higher education institutions with a dash of Christianity added in, the Evangelical college in fact could be free to create a curriculum that would actually do what it had always imagined it was called to do: to show how an academic vision truly grounded in the death, resurrection, and anticipated

---

29. Glanzer and Carpenter, "Conclusion," in Carpenter et al., eds., *Christian Higher Education*, 298.

30. Anders, *You Can Do Anything*; Hartley, *Fuzzy and the Techie*; Thomas, *Not Trivial*.

return of Christ would show higher education done differently and perhaps even inspirationally?

We could add one other practical benefit to this proposal: such a pared-down college would cost a fraction of the overheads of the current model. The Evangelical college is trapped in an arms race with larger institutions in its bid for students. This drives it to embrace ever more market-sensitive programs. But each new program generates its own financial burdens. As Michael Budde observes: "Given the cost of required facilities . . . a science curriculum just like the 'real schools' might be a millstone around the neck of a fledgling ecclesially based university, devouring all its resources and starving curricular and communal endeavors more important . . . for the distinctive purposes of such a new institution."[31] A radically scaled-back major might make good financial sense.

But perhaps Evangelical colleges are financially obligated to keep intact a diverse range of programs; perhaps they believe in some of them so profoundly that they could not imagine an Evangelical college without them. If this must be, then it is the second, weaker, version of the proposal that should be adopted. This would involve a complete overhaul of the general education/core requirements of the Christian college, and a change of attitude toward the professional disciplines. Given that most majors are no more than fifty credits, one could in theory devise a seventy-credit version of the plan I proposed above, and then still retain a range of professional majors. The core or general education would become the "primary site of implementation, coherence, and community" in embodying the mission of Christian higher education.[32] It should be upgraded from a set of sometimes disparate "requirements" to a fully integrated major, or two minors, housed in a dedicated division or department.

All faculty teaching at the institution should be required to audit this major over, say, a five-year period, so that the whole institution is aware of the nature and value of the institution's foundational curriculum. Proper course release and/or stipends should be provided for such a commitment which would be a bedrock professional development activity. As Glanzer and Carpenter observe

> Unless students take courses that address the social, economic, theological, cultural, and ethical issues that form the world in which their professions operate, they will have few resources for

31. Budde, "Assessing," in Budde and Wright, eds., *Conflicting Allegiances*, 257.
32. Fant, *Liberal Arts*, 28.

understanding and applying the Bible's call to work for justice and to love mercy . . . We might add to this that faculty teaching in these professional programs need at least the same bedrock experience as their students.[33]

In this plan it would follow that faculty in professional programs would be somewhat "let off the hook" of "integrating" faith with their classes. The futile attempt at integrating a meta-level worldview into classes where it really does not fit could be legitimately abandoned. While it is sometimes said that integrating faith and learning is not just a matter of simply praying before class or mentoring students but in professional disciplines it may well be that praying before class, or mentoring students would, in fact, be quite enough. It would certainly be better than strained and dubious references to Scripture, prooftexting, and other forms of shallow and banal "Jesusification" of the topic matter of the day. In other words, it is probably time to allow some disciplines and some professors to stop claiming that they are integrating faith and learning and to permit some professors to drop the overburdened sense that they have theologize their subject.

Theology for All

If Evangelical institutions are serious about integrating faith and learning, and if they really believe that this can and should happen in all disciplines, they should grant every faculty member time and money to gain a master's degree in theology. "Theology, when properly understood, cannot rest easily within the confines of a singular faculty."[34] If this is too exacting an idea, then theological literacy and academic biblical studies should feature as part of ongoing faculty training as much as the standard fare of faculty development offerings in pedagogical and technological training. Douglas Harink states what is surely the minimum required: "Christian scholars in other disciplines need to make some time to *read theology, traditional and contemporary*. This is not (always) the same as reading devotional literature, past and present. Rather, what is required here is some serious engagement with the ways in which Christians have thought and continue to think about God, creation and 'all things' from a center in the Church,

---

33. Glanzer and Carpenter, "Conclusion," in Carpenter et al., eds., *Christian Higher Education*, 299.

34. Glanzer et al., *Restoring the Soul*, 229.

sacraments, doctrines, and life together."[35] Glanzer and Ream make another suggestion: that Christian colleges ought to employ a full-time faculty theologian whose mission is to be theologian-in-residence for the faculty.[36]

An important part of theological literacy is attention to the ways in which interpretation of the Bible is shaped by one's own confessional and sociological position. This means that the Evangelical college also needs to be much more self-conscious about understanding the nature of Evangelical Christianity. Evangelicalism is often a movement in denial about its own existence. By using labels like "biblical" or "nondenominational," Evangelical Christianity commonly claims it is just plain old Christianity, and that it is everyone else who has added traditions or rituals to the basic message of Scripture. Evangelicals are often not aware that they are, in fact, part of a tradition like any other—a tradition that is shaped by time, place, and culture.[37] Inevitably the Evangelical college also does not often recognize itself as enmeshed in a particular tradition. It thinks of itself as just pursuing real, authentic Christianity and ignores that it is, in fact, the bearer of historical and theological freight. It treats its constituents as individual Christians but not as members of a distinct ecclesial community. It therefore often neglects to think seriously about ways in which Evangelical presuppositions have shaped both the student body and the institution, and to consider ways in which both might need to be reformed.

Just as all faculty and administrators need theological training, they also need to spend time thinking about the history and culture of the Evangelical ecclesial community in which they and their students are enmeshed. Only by doing this will the Evangelical college develop some sense of *responsibility* for the health of Evangelicalism. There is a vast literature that describes many features, ideas, and narratives in modern American Evangelical Christianity, including views of politics, gender, sexuality, race, and spiritual culture. Reading about Evangelicalism ought to be part of faculty development. Moreover, faculty ought to spend time thinking about ways in which the curriculum should *address Evangelicals as Evangelicals*. There is an extant literature that analyzes students in terms of so-called "generation studies"—IGen, ZGen, Millennials, and so on. However, do Evangelical colleges ever study their students' *religious* characteristics? Lori Kanitz recommends that "assignments need to be designed that unearth *how* our

---

35. Harink, "Taking the University to Church."
36. Glanzer et al., *Restoring the Soul*, 234.
37. On this phenomenon, see Du Mez, "What We Believe About History."

students are reading the Bible and that engage them in a healthy, critical examination of the influences shaping their interpretation of scripture and their Christian worldview."[38] Students themselves ought to learn about the strengths and weaknesses of the Evangelical tradition in both national and global contexts.

Chapel: A Central Venue for Integrating Learning with Faith

Evangelical colleges must develop a view of chapel as interwoven with the entire academic enterprise. This means faculty should take a large measure of responsibility and ownership of corporate worship. They should see its nature and culture as affecting their work in the classroom, whether they like it or not. Indeed, it is possible that chapel should stop being perceived to be "student-centered"—with the resultant attempt at ensuring the music and ethos is appealing to students—and should instead be viewed primarily as a venue in which faculty shape and participate in worship that is deemed appropriate to an academic community. Somewhat like a monastic community, the faculty at worship would extend an open and hospitable invitation to students to join them in prayer, but the worship pattern would be keyed to the permanent, not the transient, members of the academic community. As Rod Reed has argued, "Chapel is set in the context of a university, and needs to reflect its culture by contributing to students' education. It is not only a worship service; it is also worship education that can expose students to a broader view of God and the church than is represented in the individual churches from which they come."[39]

Chapel, if it remains obligatory and focused on students, should nevertheless be deeply keyed into the academic experience. There is a rich theology of worship that describes how liturgical participation is an educational, formative experience. Evangelical college chapels should take seriously the extent to which the chapel program is consciously designed to acculturate students into the Christian narrative and identity, rather than just being a program of speakers and songs. One of the major themes of James K. A. Smith is that worship may be the much more powerful a tool for teaching Christian identity and habit than a book on worldview. There is also an extensive body of writing concerning the need for worship to be

---

38. Kanitz," Improving Christian Worldview Pedagogy," 103.

39. Reed, "Power of Context," in Balzer and Reed, eds., *Building a Culture of Faith*, 129.

global and multidimensional. Evangelicalism does not generally conceptualize worship as a venue for Christian education and formation. However, among scholars and theologians of worship there is a broad consensus that worship is one of the primary venues in which Christians are enculturated into God's redemptive story, conformed into their identity as members of the body of Christ, and sent to be agents of God's mission. The Evangelical church needs to pay greater attention to worship as catechesis and formation. But if this is true, then how much more does the Evangelical college—whose whole business is Christian education—need to seriously consider the educative function of its corporate worship?[40]

This agenda requires two foci: first, the chapel *qua* chapel needs to be structured in a way that releases the full catechetical power of worship. There is little point in the chapel simply being a carbon copy of the Evangelical worship that students could experience at their church during Sunday or mid-week services. It should be consciously distinctive. This means that it should consciously expose students to the breadth of the church's historical and global liturgical traditions, styles, and worship cultures. There are, of course, limits to this: no Evangelical college is going to celebrate the Mass. But neither should the Evangelical college constrain its worship to the standard fare of contemporary Christian music. It should consciously try to correct the deficiencies of Evangelical worship. The point of doing this is not just to give students a smorgasbord of experience, but because the liturgical breadth of the global church is necessary if we are to understand our identity as members of a trans-national, trans-historical community. Moreover, since no part of the church in space and time has a complete picture of God and his actions, encountering different forms of worship is a way to broaden our knowledge, and adoration, of the eternal God. If the mission of the Evangelical college is to summon, nurture, and renew the Christian church, the kind of Christian church the college hopes to build should be modeled in microcosm in the chapel.

While diverse worship is vital, chapel should also be *structured and coherent*. "To achieve this would require more consistency and coherence in chapel planning, rather than a collection of external speakers who present individual messages that are independent from one another" that characterizes many CCCU schools.[41] Chapel should understand its mission as the same as that of the college as a whole: to help students be formed so

---

40. Glanzer et al., *Restoring the Soul*, 236.
41. Reed, "Shaping the Whole Person," 131.

that they can live a fully orbed Christian life. For example, if a college uses *worldview* language for its faculty, it should use the same paradigm for its chapel. Chapel should also be formulated to ensure that it helps teach students a Christian worldview and assessed accordingly. As worship comes to be considered through this lens it is almost inevitable that some form of liturgical pattern will surface as the best way to ensure the worship does justice to the coherence and full implications of a Christian worldview.

This observation leads to the second foci of reforming chapel. If worship could come to be seen as essential to Christian education, then it must be *integrated* with the academic curriculum of the campus. Two educational endeavors running in parallel are at best inefficient, and at worse in tension with each other. The most powerful form of Evangelical education could be one where worship comes to be seen as work, and work comes to be seen as worship. The chapel and the classroom must be integrated. As I have argued, this must be a two-way integration, not just an expectation that a standard form of Evangelical worship will set the spiritual temperature for the classroom. Learning must redound into the chapel as well as worship into the classroom. Too often chapel is seen as the catharsis from academic work.

One way to move toward this would be *structural*. The person or people with oversight of chapel should be academically qualified. They should be involved in the teaching activity of the institution. Alternatively, chapel should be overseen by a committee made up of student development *and* faculty. Faculty must step forward here and understand chapel as something that is deeply connected with their educational ambitions. Administrators must understand why faculty have a stake in the culture, programming, and liturgical form of chapel.

A further possibility presents itself. With the development of an integrated core curriculum or even of a radically simplified major, there is much greater scope for making direct connections between the content of classes and the content of chapel. Chapel could start to provide liturgical support for the academic project, offering opportunities to hear Scripture, lament, sing, and petition God on themes that are being discussed by large numbers of students within the classroom. The more that the academic program is integrated *within itself*, the more that there emerges a possibility of developing a fully integrated liturgical pattern in chapel that matches the academic program. There should, in fact, be a constant pendulum between classroom and chapel. Worship should be structured to create a hunger for knowledge—faith seeking understanding; the classroom should send students to chapel to recontextualize their learning within the worshipping community.

This proposal coheres with the liturgical turn among some proponents of worldview. For example, David Naugle has asked: "Why are there a fair number of believers who have taken all the right worldview classes, read all the right worldview books, heard all the right worldview speakers, been to all the right worldview conferences . . . and yet falter or fail when it comes to the cultivation of lifetime of Christian devotion and faithfulness?"[42] Naugle's answer is that Evangelical institutions have failed to see worldview as not only a "cognitive, but also an affective, volitional, and spiritual construct, integrated bodily."[43]

This focus on the holistic nature of worldview has led some recent treatments of worldview to lay greater emphasis on that the role played by desire, affection, and habit in enculturating people into God's reality. In turn, this has led to an emphasis on the *church* as the inculcator of the desires, habits, and identity that help people to inscribe themselves into God's unfolding story. In this construal, the sacraments, worship, and practices of the church are key to cultivating an embodied and inhabited worldview. Thus James K. A. Smith urges Christian educators to "push down through worldview to worship as the matrix from which a Christian worldview is born."[44] David Naugle concurs. "I do not recommend redoubled educational efforts as in more books to read, or lectures to hear, or conferences to attend (as valuable as these things may be). Rather, I recommend that if we wish foster the liturgical consummation of a biblical worldview, then the church and her liturgies are the key."[45]

Of course, most college chapels face a problem in realizing the full depths and possibilities of worship as formation, since they are not actually churches.[46] In particular, they do not offer the sacraments. They are also one-dimensional enterprises, missing the multigenerational nature of many churches. Perhaps it would be better to admit that the chapel *is* a church for most students, and embrace this reality, offering services on Sundays with the full pastoral and sacramental ministry that one would find in churches.

42. Naugle, "After Learning Part One" 8.
43. Naugle, "After Learning Part Two," 6.
44. Smith, *Desiring the Kingdom*, i.
45. Naugle, "After Learning Part Two," 16.
46. Glanzer et al., *Restoring the Soul*, 276.

The alternative model—one that might at first seem counter to the idea of better integrating education and worship—is to drop chapels altogether. It could be argued that the very existence of chapel on the Evangelical campus prevents the college from developing a robust educational vision that serves the church. By creating a space that *replicates* the church, but in a hollowed-out form, does the Evangelical college invite students to disassociate from local congregations? Does it provide an experience of ecclesial community so *unlike* the church—no sacraments, no multigenerational community, an unclear model of pastoral oversight—that it in fact does little to help students grow into lifelong membership of the church, and to understand the church as the primary agent of God's mission in the world? Is chapel, in other words, a simulacrum of a church that is sufficiently church-like to absorb the spiritual energy of the campus but not sufficiently church-like to help students become part of the people of God? This argument might find support in the evidence that campus chapel can be *detrimental* to student faith. If the Evangelical college is aiming to help students prepare to live Christianly for a lifetime, how helpful is it to offer a daily, large-scale worship experience?

Would the Evangelical college better spend it money by building robust partnerships with local churches? Could it pay a team of pastors to act as part-time chaplains to the whole university? Could it partner with local churches to establish mentoring and hospitality networks with local families? Instead of providing its own chapel, with the expense of infrastructure, personnel, audio-visual equipment, and so on, could the Evangelical colleges simply provide transport to local churches on a Sunday morning? Alternatively, could a parachurch establish a presence on campus? It might seem odd to suggest that a group like Inter-Varsity Fellowship or Campus Crusade for Christ (now Cru) set up shop on the campus of an Evangelical college. But it might in fact *sharpen* the Christian identity of the institution. It is possible that the spiritual paraphernalia of the Christian college promotes a complacency. It might be useful to have a student group with a sharper vision of evangelism and discipleship. Such a group would also allow Evangelical college students to plug in to broader student networks, meeting Evangelical colleges at non-Christian institutions, and breaking the artificiality of the Christian college "bubble"—which will burst sooner or later anyway.

The college and local churches

As well as establishing partnerships with local churches to provide pastoral support and Christian community to students, the ecclesially focused Evangelical college should of course think about other ways to build lived relationships with local churches that go beyond merely seeing them as places that can send students or money. If the Evangelical college came to see itself as a place where faith learns, then it ought to work hard to develop partnerships and opportunities for local Christians to learn. As with education in general, it could be quipped that Evangelical education is wasted on the young! It is as life experience accrues that many Christians find they have increasing appetite to engage in deeper study of Christianity and culture. The Evangelical college ought to position itself as a key resource for local churches—a center for Christian education. Could local churches outsource some element of adult education to the Evangelical college? This might involve lifelong learning programs, nonaccredited initiatives, or specific partnerships with local churches in which the college offers adult education programs, perhaps on key themes of Christian concern. The Evangelical college ought to be the cathedral of learning for the surrounding "diocese"—a space in which all Christians can continue to grow in their faith and vocation as they learn more about God, his world, and his church. In this Evangelical colleges should become seminaries for the laity. George Marsden, long a champion of a more cerebral form of faith-learning integration, has more recently glimpsed this alternative vision:

> Most CCCU schools are, in effect, para-church institutions. They build their own identities, but they are also intermeshed in a web of relationships with other church and para-church organizations that make up the complex entity of evangelicalism. Since these institutions are all voluntary, they are not easy to reform. In such a setting Christian colleges and universities might see their roles as to be that of gently guiding and reforming their supporting church communities by training laypeople (as well as clergy) who eventually can provide mature leadership in practicing their faith in an alien world.[47]

---

47. Marsden, "Moving Up," in Joeckel and Chesnes, eds., *Christian College Phenomenon*, 363.

CONCLUSION

Where are faith and learning to be integrated? In their guidebook to Evangelical education. Badley and Allan propose three possibilities: faith and learning can be integrated in the curriculum, in the student, and in the professor. They opt, as do many others, for the professor. Hal Poe adds a fourth option. He argues "the professions represent the point where people integrate their education."[48]

If these are the only four options, then this book has proposed that the *curriculum* must be the place where faith and learning meet. The responsibility for ensuring a Christ-centered learning experience rests with the college as a whole, not with individual faculty. Indeed, individual professors are handed a poisoned chalice when asked to teach a set of basically secular, segmented disciplines "from a Christian perspective." We have seen the dispiriting results that can arise from this scenario. At best there is a fragmented and disjointed picture of Christianity; at worst Christianity is trivialized and distorted. The curriculum of the Evangelical college should be so carefully constructed to fulfill the Christian aims of the college that it would really be impossible for a professor *not* to integrate faith and learning. As I have argued, this would require a substantial, if not radical, revision of the Evangelical college.

But the Evangelical college also needs to go beyond this internal "integration." Harry Lee Poe is right to suggest that the ultimate integration is *beyond* the college in the lives and activities of its graduates. However, in opting for "the professions" he identifies the wrong loci of integration. Indeed, I have argued that the importation of professional training into the Evangelical college poses many challenges to maintaining any sense of distinctive Christian education. It tends to dull the ability of the college to adopt a posture of biblically informed critical and prophetic distance from the political economy of the modern nation-state. Instead, I have proposed that the ultimate place in which faith and learning should be integrated is *the church.*

Identifying the church as the locus of integration will always sound odd when the concept of integration is assumed to be about infusing faith into learning. In such a paradigm, to argue that the church is the site of integration would be to argue that faith should be integrated in the one

---

48. Harry Lee Poe, "The Gospel, Worldview, and Christian Higher Education," in Dockery, ed., *Faith and Learning,* 81.

place that is assumed to already be full of faith and the faithful. But, as I have contended, the Evangelical college should stop seeing faith as its distinctive contribution to higher education and start viewing learning as its distinctive contribution to the church. The church must be the site of integration because the church—particularly the Evangelical church of North America—needs the learning that the Evangelical college is uniquely positioned to offer.

The Evangelical college is not configured to properly advance its ecclesial vocation. It needs a new integrated curriculum, a greater commitment to deepening the individual and communal theological literacy and missiological vision of the faculty, a reoriented understanding of the relationship between academics and cocurricular activities such as chapel, and, most of all, urgent attention to the insidious patterns of secularization at work on its campus—be they the market, the nation, or the Evangelical tradition itself. The Evangelical college—from the board of trustees down—must plot itself more firmly within the Christian narrative, and to learn to see the Christian college itself from a Christian worldview. It must ask urgent questions about how the Evangelical college might live faithfully and prophetically within the unfolding kingdom of God.

None of this is easy; much of it may even seem impossible. But to desist is to squander the great opportunities presented to us, and to allow our institutions, and our churches, to continue their secularizing drift. Such a radical reformation would carry great risk, but to do nothing would be a scandal.

Bibliography

Agee, Bob R. and Henry, Douglas V., eds. *Faithful Learning and the Christian Scholarly Vocation*. Grand Rapids: Eerdmans, 2003.
Alleman, Nathan F. "The Christian College Advantage? The Impact of Christian Versus Secular Training Among Faculty at Christian Colleges and Universities." *Journal of Research on Christian Education* 24 (2015) 252–70.
Allen, Patrick, and Kenneth Badley. *Echoes of Insight: Past Perspectives and the Future of Christian Higher Education*. Abilene, TX: Abilene Christian University Press, 2017.
———. *Faith and Learning: A Practical Guide for Faculty*. Abilene, TX: Leafwood Publishers and Abilene Christian University Press, 2014.
Anders, George. *You Can Do Anything: The Surprising Power of a "Useless" Liberal Arts Education*. New York: Little, Brown and Company, 2017.
Arizona Christian University. "Mission." https://www.arizonachristian.edu/about/mission/.
Asbury University. "Foundations." https://www.asbury.edu/about/offices/registrar/foundations/.
Azusa Pacific University. "At a Glance." https://www.apu.edu/advancement/profile/.
Badley, Ken. "Clarifying 'Faith-Learning Integration': Essentially Contested Concepts and the Concept-Conception Distinction." *Journal of Education and Christian Belief* 13 (2009) 7–17.
———. "The Faith/Learning Integration Movement in Christian Higher Education: Slogan or Substance?" *Journal of Research on Christian Education* 3 (1994) 13–33.
Baker, Vicki L., et al., "Where Are They Now?" *Liberal Education* 98 (2012) 48–53.
Balzer, Cary, and Rod Reed, eds. *Building a Culture of Faith: University-Wide Partnerships for Spiritual Formation*. Abilene, TX: Abilene Christian University Press, 2012.
Bartholomew, Craig G. *Contours of the Kuyperian Tradition: A Systematic Introduction*. Downers Grove, IL: IVP Academic, 2017.
Bauckham, Richard. *The Theology of the Book of Revelation*. New York: Cambridge University Press, 1993.
Bayly, Tim. "The Scandal of the Evangelical College . . ." January 7, 2016. http://baylyblog.com/blog/2016/01/scandal-evangelical-college.
Bebbington, D. W. *Evangelicalism in Modern Britain a History from the 1730s to the 1980s*. London: Routledge, 1993.
Beck, Albert R. "All Truth Is God's Truth: The Life and Ideas of Frank E. Gaebelein." PhD diss., Baylor University, 2008.
Beers, Stephen. *The Soul of a Christian University: A Field Guide for Educators*. Abilene, TX: Abilene Christian University Press, 2008.

Bibliography

Bethel University. "Mission, Vision, Values." https://www.bethel.edu/about/mission-vision-values.

Bilbro, Jeffrey, et al., eds. *The Liberating Arts: Why We Need Liberal Arts Education.* Walden, NY: Plough, 2023.

Bonzo, J. Matthew, and Michael Stevens, eds. *After Worldview.* Sioux Center, IA: Dordt College Press, 2009.

Bower, Lorraine. "Faith-Learning Interaction in Graphic Design Courses." *Christian Higher Education* 9 (2010) 5–27.

Bradley, Ian C. *Abide with Me: The World of Victorian Hymns.* Chicago: GIA, 1997.

Bratt, James. "Why I'm Sick of Every Square Inch." https://blog.reformedjournal.com/2013/10/12/why-im-sick-of-every-square-inch/.

Bratt, James D., and Mark A. Noll. *Abraham Kuyper: Modern Calvinist, Christian Democrat.* Grand Rapids: Eerdmans, 2013.

Brenneman, Todd M. *Homespun Gospel: The Triumph of Sentimentality in Contemporary American Evangelicalism.* Oxford: Oxford University Press, 2013.

Budde, Michael L., and John Wright, eds. *Conflicting Allegiances: The Church-Based University In A Liberal Democratic Society.* Grand Rapids: Brazos, 2004.

Burtchaell, James Tunstead. *The Dying of the Light: The Disengagement of Colleges and Universities from Their Christian Churches.* Grand Rapids: Eerdmans, 1998.

Burton, Larry D., and Constance C. Nwosu. "Student Perceptions of the Integration of Faith, Learning, and Practice In an Educational Methods Course." *Journal of Research on Christian Education* 12 (2003) 101–35.

Calvin Institute of Christian Worship. "Dru Johnson on Bible Literacy, Fluency, and Engagement." https://worship.calvin.edu/resources/resource-library/dru-johnson-on-bible-literacy-fluency-and-engagement/.

Campbellsville University. "Are Christian-Affiliated Universities Equipping Business Students from a Biblical Perspective?" August 3, 2017. https://www.campbellsville.edu/blog/christian-affiliated-universities-equipping-business-students-biblical-perspective/.

Carpenter, Joel A. "Reawakening Evangelical Intellectual Life. A Christian Scholar's Review." February 8, 2022. https://christianscholars.com/reawakening-evangelical-intellectual-life-a-christian-scholars-review/.

———. "Response to Harry Fernhout." *Christian Higher Education* 1 (2002) 273–80.

Carpenter, Joel, et al., eds. *Christian Higher Education: A Global Reconnaissance.* Grand Rapids: Eerdmans, 2014.

Carpenter, Joel A., and Kenneth W. Shipps. *Making Higher Education Christian: The History and Mission of Evangelical Colleges in America.* Grand Rapids: Eerdmans, 1987.

Carson, D. A. *Christ and Culture Revisited.* Grand Rapids: Eerdmans, 2012.

Carter, Heath W., and Laura Porter. *Turning Points in the History of American Evangelicalism.* Grand Rapids: Eerdmans, 2017.

CBS Minnesota. "Trump on Evangelicals. They Really Love Me." February 1, 2016. https://www.cbsnews.com/minnesota/news/trump-on-evangelicals-they-really-love-me/.

CCCU. "About." https://www.cccu.org/about/.

———. "Networking Grants." https://www.cccu.org/campus-grants-networking-grants/.

———. "Our Institutions." https://www.cccu.org/institutions/.

Clapp, Rodney R. *A Peculiar People: The Church as Culture in a Post-Christian Society.* Downers Grove, IL: IVP Academic, 1996.

Bibliography

Colorado Christian University. "CCU—A military-focused school." https://www.ccu.edu/ccu/military/.
Corban University. "Who We Are." https://www.corban.edu/about/history/who-we-are-and-who-we-aspire-to-be.
Cornerstone University. "Employment." https://www.cornerstone.edu/about/employment/.
Cosgrove, Preston B. "Variations on a Theme: Convergent Thinking and the Integration of Faith and Learning. *Christian Higher Education* 14 (2015) 229–43.
Cox, Daniel A. "Rise of Conspiracies Reveals an Evangelical Divide in the GOP." February 1, 2021. https://www.americansurveycenter.org/rise-of-conspiracies-reveal-an-evangelical-divide-in-the-gop/.
Crisp, Thomas M., et al., eds. *Christian Scholarship in the Twenty-First Century: Prospects and Perils*. Grand Rapids: Eerdmans, 2014.
Davis, Jeffry C., et al., eds. *Liberal Arts for the Christian Life*. Wheaton, IL: Crossway, 2012.
Dockery, David S., ed. *Faith and Learning: A Handbook for Christian Higher Education*. Nashville, TN: B&H Academic, 2012.
Dockery, David S., and Christopher W. Morgan, eds. *Christian Higher Education: Faith, Teaching, and Learning in the Evangelical Tradition*. Wheaton, IL: Crossway, 2018.
Dockery, David S., and Trevin Wax. *Christian Worldview Handbook*. Nashville: Holman Reference, 2019.
Downing, Crystal L. "Imbricating Faith and Learning: The Architectonics of Christian Scholarship." In *Scholarship and Christian Faith: Enlarging the Conversation*, edited by Douglas Jacobsen and Rhonda Hustedt Jacobsen, 33–43. New York: Oxford University Press, 2004.
Dreher, Rod. "Eric Metaxas's American Apocalypse." December 10, 2020. https://www.theamericanconservative.com/eric-metaxas-trump-bloodshed-american-apocalypse-live-not-by-lies/.
Du Mez, Kristin Kobes. "What We Believe About History." May 27, 2021. https://www.nytimes.com/2021/05/27/special-series/kristin-kobes-du-mez-what-we-believe-about-history.html.
East, Brad. "Once More, Church and Culture." https://mereorthodoxy.com/once-more-church-and-culture.
Eaton, Philip W. *Engaging the Culture, Changing the World: The Christian University in a Post-Christian World*. Downers Grove, IL: IVP Academic, 2011.
Emerging Scholars Blog. "Introducing Kuyper's 'Sphere Sovereignty.'" September 26, 2014. https://blog.emergingscholars.org/2014/09/sphere-sovereignty/.
Empsall, Nathan. "The Blasphemy of Comparing Trump to Jesus Christ." April 6, 2023. https://time.com/6269313/trump-jesus-comparisons-blasphemy/.
Fant, Gene C. *The Liberal Arts: A Student's Guide. Reclaiming the Christian Intellectual Tradition*. Wheaton, IL: Crossway, 2012.
Fea, John. *Believe Me: The Evangelical Road to Donald Trump*. 1st ed. Grand Rapids: Eerdmans, 2018.
———. "What is the State of the Evangelical Mind on Christian College Campuses?" *Christian Scholar's Review* 47 (2018) 341–44.
Fea, John, et al. *Confessing History*. South Bend, IN: University of Notre Dame Press, 2010.
Firmin, Michael W., and Krista Merrick Gilson. "Mission Statement Analysis of CCCU Member Institutions." *Christian Higher Education* 9 (2009) 60–70.
Gaffin, Richard. "Profile: Nick Van Til." *Christian Educators Journal* (1982) 23–24.

Bibliography

Galli, Mark. "The Anvil of the Evangelical Mind: Schools and scholars can help the Christ-centered movement become all the more Jesusy." *Christianity Today* 63 (2019) 62.

Gehrz, Chris. "Christian Higher Ed Is Not the CCCU." *The Pietist Schoolman*, September 28, 2015. https://pietistschoolman.com/2015/09/28/christian-higher-ed-is-not-the-cccu/.

———. "'Nothing for Your Journey': The Future of the Christian Liberal Arts." *The Pietist Schoolman*, April 21, 2020. https://pietistschoolman.com/2020/04/19/nothing-for-your-journey-the-future-of-the-christian-liberal-arts/.

Gehrz, Christopher, ed. *The Pietist Vision of Christian Higher Education: Forming Whole and Holy Persons.* Downers Grove, IL: IVP Academic, 2015.

Glanzer, Perry L. "The Secular University's Problematic Justifications for General Education: But Christians Need to Provide Better Alternatives and Not Simply a Better Justification." June 16, 2023. https://christianscholars.com/the-secular-universitys-problematic-justifications-for-general-education-but-christians-need-to-provide-better-alternatives-and-not-simply-a-better-justification/.

———. "Why We Should Discard 'the Integration of Faith and Learning': Rearticulating the Mission of the Christian Scholar." *Journal of Education & Christian Belief* 12 (2008) 41–51.

Glanzer, Perry L., and Todd C. Ream. *Christianity and Moral Identity in Higher Education: Becoming Fully Human.* New York: Palgrave Macmillan, 2014.

Glanzer, Perry L., and Nathan F. Alleman, eds. *The Outrageous Idea of Christian Teaching.* New York: Oxford University Press, 2019.

Glanzer, Perry L., et al. *Restoring the Soul of the University: Unifying Christian Higher Education in a Fragmented Age.* Downers Grove, IL: IVP Academic, 2017.

Gordon College. "The Gordon College 3-2 Engineering Program." https://www.gordon.edu/download/pages/Gordon%20College%203-2%20Program%20Fall2012.pdf.

Gould, Paul M., and J. P. Moreland. *The Outrageous Idea of the Missional Professor, International Edition.* Eugene, OR: Wipf & Stock, 2019.

Grace College. "Educational Values." https://online.grace.edu/about/mission-values/.

Green, J. D. "On the Evangelical Mind and Consulting the Faithful." *Christian Scholar's Review* 47 (2018) 335–39.

Hamilton, Michael S. "Reflection and Response: The Elusive Idea of Christian Scholarship." *Christian Scholar's Review* 31 (2001) 13–30.

Hannibal La-Grange University. "Vision, Mission and Core Values." https://www.hlg.edu/about-hlgu/vision-mission-core-values/.

Harnick, George. "A Historian's Comment on the Use of Abraham Kuyper's Idea of Sphere Sovereignty." *Journal of Markets and Morality* 5 (2002) 277–84.

Harink, Douglas. "Taking the University to Church: The Role of Theology in the Christian University Curriculum." *Christian Scholar's Review* 28 (1999) 389–410.

Harris, Robert A. *The Integration of Faith and Learning: A Worldview Approach.* Eugene, OR: Cascade, 2004.

Hart, D. G. "Christian Scholars, Secular Universities, and the Problem with Antithesis." *Christian Scholars' Review* 30 (2001) 383–402.

Hartley, Scott. *The Fuzzy and the Techie: Why the Liberal Arts Will Rule the Digital World.* Boston: Houghton Mifflin Harcourt, 2017.

Hasker, William. "Faith-Learning Integration: An Overview." *Christian Scholar's Review* 21 (1993) 244–46.

Bibliography

Hawthorne, John. "Christian Colleges are Losers in the Culture Wars." October 10, 2022. https://johnhawthorne.substack.com/p/christian-colleges-are-losers-in.

———. *The Fearless Christian University*. Grand Rapids: Eerdmans, 2025.

———. "On Not Fighting the Culture Wars." September 6, 2023. https://johnhawthorne.substack.com/p/on-not-fighting-culture-wars-3f7.

———. "Three Problematic Metaphors in Christian Higher Education." https://johnhawthorne.substack.com/p/three-problematic-metaphors-in-christian-higher-education.

Heie, Harold, and David L. Wolfe, eds. *The Reality of Christian Learning: Strategies for Faith-Discipline Integration*. Grand Rapids: Eerdmans, 1987.

Heller, Jack. "Divine Diversity In the Study of Literature and Writing." https://www.huntington.edu/uploads/page/Heller.pdf.

———. "Christian College Professor Flunks Worldview Tests." November 8, 2011. https://jackheller.wordpress.com/2011/11/08/christian-college-professor-flunks-christian-worldview-tests/.

Henck, Anita Fitzgerald Henck. "Walking the Tightrope: Christian Colleges and Universities in a Time of Change." *Christian Higher Education*, 10 (2011) 196–214.

Henderson, Roger "Kuyper's Inch." *Pro Rege* 36 (2008) 12–14.

Herrity, Andrew. "What If We're Graduating Utilitarians?" *Christian Business Academy Review* (2017) 133–47.

Holder, Melvin. "Comprehensive Biblical Integration." *Christian Business Academy Review* (2016) 41–49.

Holmes, Arthur F. *The Idea of a Christian College*. Grand Rapids: Eerdmans, 1987.

Hughes, Richard T., and William B. Adrian, eds. *Models for Christian Higher Education* Grand Rapids: Eerdmans, 1997.

Hunter, James Davison. *To Change the World: The Irony, Tragedy, and Possibility of Christianity in the Late Modern World*. New York: Oxford University Press, 2010.

Jacobsen, Douglas, and Rhonda Hustedt Jacobsen, eds. *Scholarship and Christian Faith: Enlarging the Conversation*. New York: Oxford University Press, 2004.

Jaschick, Scott. "Professor's Job Endangered for Teaching About Race." February 9, 2023. https://www.insidehighered.com/news/2023/02/20/professors-job-endangered-teaching-about-race.

Jenkins, Jack. "Survey: More Than a Quarter of White Evangelicals Believe Core QAnon Conspiracy Theory." February 11, 2021. https://religionnews.com/2021/02/11/survey-more-than-a-quarter-of-white-evangelicals-believe-core-qanon-conspiracy-theory/.

Joeckel, Samuel, and Thomas Chesnes, eds. *The Christian College Phenomenon: Inside America's Fastest Growing Institutions of Higher Learning*. Abilene, TX: Abilene Christian University Press, 2012.

Johnstone, David M. "Christian Higher Education at the Start of the 21st Century: A Review Essay." *Christian Higher Education* 14 (2015) 177–81.

Kaak, Paul. "Academic Faith Integration: Introduction to a New Section Within Christian Higher Education." *Christian Higher Education* 15 (2016) 189–99.

Kanitz, Lori. "Improving Christian Worldview Pedagogy: Going Beyond Mere Christianity." *Christian Higher Education* (2005) 99–108.

Kaul, Corina R., et al. "Predicting Faculty Integration of Faith and Learning." *Christian Higher Education* 16 (2017) 172–87.

Bibliography

Kidd, Thomas S. *Who Is An Evangelical? The History of a Movement in Crisis*. New Haven: Yale University Press, 2020.

King, Don W. *Take Every Thought Captive: Forty Years of the Christian Scholar's Review*. Abilene, TX: Abilene Christian University Press, 2016.

Kreider, Alan. *Worship and Mission after Christendom*. Colorado Springs: Paternoster, 2009.

Kruse, Kevin M. *One Nation Under God: How Corporate America Invented Christian America*. New York: Basic Books, 2015.

Kuyper, Abraham. *Encyclopedia of Sacred Theology: Its Principles*. Translated by J. Hendrik De Vries. New York: Charles Scribner's Sons, 1898.

———. "Sphere Sovereignty. A Public address delivered at the inauguration of the Free University, Oct. 20, 1880." Translated by George Kamps. https://media.thegospelcoalition.org/wp-content/uploads/2017/06/24130543/SphereSovereignty_English.pdf.

Laats, Adam. *Fundamentalist U: Keeping the Faith in American Higher Education*. New York: Oxford University Press, 2018.

Labberton, Mark. "Political Dealing: The Crisis of Evangelicalism." https:www.fuller.edu/posts/political-dealing-the-crisis-of-evangelicalism/.

Lewis, C. S. *The Weight of Glory*. New York: HarperCollins, 2001.

Litfin, Duane. *Conceiving the Christian College*. Grand Rapids: Eerdmans, 2004.

Longman, Karen A. *Diversity Matters: Race, Ethnicity, and the Future of Christian Higher Education*. Abilene, TX: Abilene Christian University Press, 2017.

———. *Thriving in Leadership: Strategies for Making a Difference in Christian Higher Education*. Abilene, TX: Abilene Christian University Press, 2012.

Lyon, L., et al. "Making sense of a 'religious'" university: Faculty adaptations and opinions at Brigham Young, Baylor, Notre Dame, and Boston College." *Review of Religious Research* 43 (2002) 326–48.

Lyons, Sierra. "When Christian Colleges Fire 'Woke' Professors Who Will Stop Them?" https://sojo.net/articles/when-christian-colleges-fire-woke-professors-who-will-stop-them.

Mannoia, V. James, Jr. "Christian Higher Education: An Education That Liberates." *Christian Higher Education* 14 (2015) 87–97.

———. *Christian Liberal Arts: An Education That Goes Beyond*. Lanham, MD: Rowman & Littlefield, 2000.

Marsden, George M. *The Soul of the American University Revisited: From Protestant to Postsecular*. New York: Oxford University Press, 2021.

———. "The State of Evangelical Christian Scholarship." *Christian Scholar's Review* 17 (1988) 347–60.

Marsden, George M., and Bradley J. Longfield, eds. *The Secularization of the Academy*. New York: Oxford University Press, 1992.

Marsh, Charles. *Wayward Christian Soldiers: Freeing the Gospel from Political Captivity*. New York: Oxford University Press, 2007.

McKenna, David L. *Christ-Centered Higher Education: Memory, Meaning, and Momentum for the Twenty-First Century*. Eugene, OR: Wipf & Stock, 2012.

McKenzie, Robert Tracy. "The Vocation of The Christian Historian: Re-Envisioning Our Calling, Reconnecting With the Church." *Fides et Historia* 45 (2013) 1–13.

Meadors, Edward P., ed. *Where Wisdom May Be Found: The Eternal Purpose of Christian Higher Education*. Eugene, OR: Pickwick, 2019.

Bibliography

Mid-America Nazarene. "Points of Pride." https://www.mnu.edu/about-us/points-of-pride/.

Miller, Eric. "Anti-Intellectualism and the Integration of Faith and Learning." *Christian Scholar's Review* 47 (2018) 329–34.

Moltmann, Jürgen. *Theology of Hope*. London: Harper and Row, 1967.

Montreat College. "Vision, Mission. Statement of Faith, and Community Life Covenant." https://www.montreat.edu/about/mission/.

Moreton, Bethany. *To Serve God and Wal-Mart: The Making of Christian Free Enterprise*. Cambridge: Harvard University Press, 2010.

Moroney, S. "Where Faith and Learning Intersect: Re-Mapping the Contemporary Terrain." *Christian Scholars Review* 43 (2014) 139–55.

Naugle, David K. "After Learning: The Liturgical Consummation of Worldviews Part One." https://www3.dbu.edu/naugle/pdf/AfterLearningLiturgicalConsummationPart1.pdf.

———. "After Learning: The Liturgical Consummation of Worldviews Part Two." https://www3.dbu.edu/naugle/pdf/AfterLearningLiturgicalConsummationPart2.pdf.

———. "Scrutinizing a Scandal: A Christian Worldview Analysis of a Christian College Professor Who Flunks Christian Worldview Tests and Doesn't Teach from a Christian Worldview." https://www3.dbu.edu/naugle/pdf/ScrutinizingaScandal.pdf.

———. *Worldview: The History of a Concept*. Grand Rapids: Eerdmans, 2002.

Newbigin, Lesslie. *Foolishness to the Greeks: The Gospel and Western Culture*. Grand Rapids: Eerdmans, 1986.

———. *The Gospel in a Pluralist Society*. Grand Rapids: Eerdmans, 1989.

Newman, Elizabeth. *Divine Abundance: Leisure. The Basis of Academic Culture*. Eugene, OR: Cascade, 2018.

Nienhuis, David R. "The Problem of Evangelical Biblical Illiteracy." January 1, 2010. https://www.modernreformation.org/resources/articles/the-problem-of-evangelical-biblical-illiteracy.

Noll, Mark A. *Jesus Christ and the Life of the Mind*. Grand Rapids: Eerdmans, 2013.

———. *The Scandal of the Evangelical Mind*. Grand Rapids: Eerdmans, 1995.

Noll, Mark A., et al., eds. *Evangelicals: Who They Have Been, Are Now, and Could Be*. Grand Rapids: Eerdmans, 2019.

North Central University, "About." https://www.northcentral.edu/about/.

Northwest Nazarene University. "Crossing the Bridge." July 23, 2019. https://www.nnu.edu/news/crossing-the-bridge.

Northwest University. "Mission and Values." https://www.northwestu.edu/about/mission.

Nwosu, Constance Chibuzo. "Integration of Faith and Learning in Christian Higher Education: Professional Development of Teachers and Classroom Implementation." PhD diss., Andrews University, 1999. https://digitalcommons.andrews.edu/dissertations/607.

Olree, Andy. "Review of James K. Smith, *Desiring the Kingdom*." *Journal of Faith and the Academy* 2 (2009) 24.

Orr, James. *The Christian View of God and the World as Centering in the Incarnation*. New York: Scribner, 1887.

Page, Nick. *And Now Let's Move into a Time of Nonsense: Why Worship Songs Are Failing the Church*. Waynesboro, GA: Authentic, 2004.

Bibliography

Patterson, James A. "Boundary Maintenance in Evangelical Christian Higher Education: A Case Study of the Council for Christian Colleges & Universities." *Christian Higher Education* 4 (2005) 41–56

Rampersad, Dave. "The Meaning of the Christian University." *Journal of Faith and the Academy* 1 (2008) 25–38.

Ream, Todd C. *Beyond Integration: Inter/Disciplinary Possibilities for the Future of Christian Higher Education.* Abilene, TX: Abilene Christian University Press, 2012.

Ream, Todd C., and Perry Glanzer. *The Idea of a Christian College: A Reexamination for Today's University.* Eugene, OR: Cascade, 2013.

Ream, Todd C., and Perry F. Glanzer. *Christian Faith and Scholarship: An Exploration of Contemporary Developments."* ASHE Higher Education Report 33, no. 2. Hoboken, NJ: Jossey-Bass, 2007.

Reed, Rodney P. "Shaping the Whole Person: A Measure of Institutional Intentionality for Evangelical Spiritual Formation in North American Christian Higher Education." PhD diss., University of Bristol, 2012.

Ringenberg, William C. *The Christian College: A History of Protestant Higher Education in America.* Grand Rapids: Baker Academic, 2006.

San Diego Christian University. "Why San Diego Christian University?" https://sdcc.edu/why-sdcc/.

Schaeffer, Francis A. *How Should We Then Live? The Rise and Decline of Western Thought and Culture.* Wheaton, IL: Crossway, 2005.

Schreiner, Laurie, ed. *Re-Imagining Christian Higher Education.* New York: Routledge, 2018.

Schuurman, Derek C. "Forging a Christian College Core Curriculum." April 9, 2021. https://christianscholars.com/forging-a-christian-college-core-curriculum/.

Schuurman, Derek. "Approaches to Christian Education: From Elusive Towards a Larger and Deeper Approach." *Pro Rege* 44 (2016) 14–20.

Shellnutt, Kate. "Can Wheaton College Require ROTC Program Be Run By Christians?" *Christianity Today.* November 24, 2014. https://www.christianitytoday.com/news/2014/november/can-wheaton-college-require-rotc-program-run-christians.html.

Slisco, Aila. "White Evangelicals More Open to Political Violence Than Non-Christians." October 26, 2023. https://www.newsweek.com/evangelicals-political-violence-non-christians-1838384.

Smietana, Bob. "Wheaton College Suspends Hijab-Wearing Professor After 'Same God' Comment." *Christianity Today,* December 5, 2015. https://www.christianitytoday.com/news/2015/december/wheaton-college-hijab-professor-same-god-larycia-hawkins.html.

Smith, David I., and James K. A. Smith, eds. *Teaching and Christian Practices: Reshaping Faith and Learning.* Grand Rapids: Eerdmans, 2011.

Smith, James K. A. *Desiring the Kingdom: Worship, Worldview, and Cultural Formation.* Grand Rapids: Baker Academic, 2009.

Southeastern University. "About." https://seu.edu/about/.

Southern Wesleyan University. "Who We Are." https://www.swu.edu/about/who-we-are/.

Sweeney, Douglas A. *The American Evangelical Story: A History of the Movement.* Grand Rapids: Baker Academic, 2005.

Thomas, Laurie Endicott. *Not Trivial: How Studying the Traditional Liberal Arts Can Set You Free.* Leawood, KS: Freedom of Speech, 2013.

Bibliography

Tocqueville, Alexis de. *Democracy in America*. New York: Everyman's Library, 1994.

Tolbert, Dawn. "An Exploration of the Use of Branding to Shape Institutional Image in the Marketing Activities of Faith-Based Higher Education Institutions." *Christian Higher Education* 13 (2014) 233–49.

Trueman, Carl. "The Real Scandal of the Evangelical Mind." March 1, 2010. https://www.9marks.org/article/real-scandal-evangelical-mind/.

Tuininga, Matthew J. "Abraham Kuyper and the Social Order: Principles for Christian Liberalism." *Journal of Markets and Morality* (2020) 337–61.

VanZanten, Susan. *Joining the Mission: A Guide for New Faculty*. Grand Rapids: Eerdmans 2011.

Walsh, Brian J., and J. Richard Middleton. *The Transforming Vision: Shaping a Christian World View*. Downers Grove, IL: IVP Academic, 1984.

Wax, Trevin. "Rebirth of Virtue: An Interview with N. T. Wright." https://www.thegospelcoalition.org/blogs/trevin-wax/the-rebirth-of-virtue-an-interview-with-n-t-wright/.

Weber, Timothy P. *On the Road to Armageddon: How Evangelicals Became Israel's Best Friend*. Grand Rapids: Baker Academic, 2004.

Wells, Cynthia. "Renewing Our Shared Purpose: Considering Boyer's General Education Vision for Christian Colleges." *Christian Higher Education: An International Journal of Research, Theory, and Practice* 13 (2014) 43–60.

Wehner, Peter. "The Evangelical Church Is Breaking Apart." October 24, 2021. https://www.theatlantic.com/ideas/archive/2021/10/evangelical-trump-christians-politics/620469/.

Wheaton College. "Department of Military Service—Army ROTC." https://www.wheaton.edu/academics/programs/rotc/.

Wierenga, Audrey. "Cornerstone Students Dive Deep into Austrian Economics. https://www.cornerstone.edu/cornerstone-students-dive-deep-into-austrian-economics-at-mises-university/.

William Jessup University. "Mission, Vision, Statement of Faith." https://jessup.edu/about/mission/.

Wittmer, Michael Eugene. "Analysis and Critique of 'Christ the Transformer of Culture' in the Thought of H. Richard Niebuhr." PhD diss., Calvin College, 2000.

Wolterstorff, Nicholas. *Educating for Shalom: Essays on Christian Higher Education*. Grand Rapids: Eerdmans, 2004.

Woodrow, James. "Institutional Image: Secular and Marketing Influences on Christian Higher Education." *Christian Higher Education* 3 (2004) 115–25.

Wright, Christopher J. H. *The Mission of God: Unlocking the Bible's Grand Narrative*. Downers Grove, IL: IVP Academic, 2006.

Wright, N. T. *Paul in Fresh Perspective*. Minneapolis: Fortress, 2005.

Wright, N. T., and Michal F. Bird. *The New Testament in Its World: An Introduction to the History, Literature, and Theology of the First Christians*. Grand Rapids: Zondervan Academic, 2019.

Yerxa, Donald A. "That Embarrassing Dream: Big Questions and the Limits of History." *Fides et Historia* 39 (2007) 53–65.

Yoder, Michael L. "Classroom Advocacy? A Christian Pacifist's Dilemma." *Christian Higher Education* 9 (2009) 82–102.

www.ingramcontent.com/pod-product-compliance
Lightning Source LLC
Chambersburg PA
CBHW030901170426
43193CB00009BA/698